THE FAST AND HEALTHY LOW CHOLESTEROL COOKBOOK

HEFSEH SOTHARLEND

INTRODUCTION

Welcome to "The Fast and Healthy Low Cholesterol Cookbook"—a guide to heart-healthy eating, understanding the connection between cholesterol and your diet, and a treasure trove of flavorful recipes that will make your transition to a healthier lifestyle not just feasible, but also enjoyable. The aim of this book is to ease your journey towards a healthier lifestyle, whether you are new to cooking, new to the concept of low cholesterol diet, or simply looking for some fresh culinary inspiration.

Our bodies need cholesterol to build healthy cells, but too much of it can have adverse effects, leading to health issues such as heart disease. However, managing cholesterol levels doesn't have to mean bland, joyless meals. Indeed, this cookbook will show you that you can enjoy delicious, satisfying meals without compromising your health or your taste buds.

The first chapter of this book, "The Cholesterol-Diet Connection," will help you understand the science behind cholesterol, its impact on our bodies, and how our diet choices can affect our health. For those wondering how to merge theory into practical application, worry no more. This chapter will guide you on how to incorporate heart-healthy eating principles into your diet, offering you insights on what to eat and what to limit. You will discover why saturated and trans fats are important to consider in your dietary choices, how to limit your intake of these fats, and understand the recommended daily dietary cholesterol guidelines. Additionally, it will walk you through the role of supplements and exercise in maintaining a balanced lifestyle.

As you make your way through this book, you'll learn about the impact of diet on our cholesterol levels, find out how to set up a low-cholesterol kitchen, and how to maintain a pantry that promotes heart-healthy eating. You'll gain knowledge about key ingredients that help fight cholesterol, and you'll acquire practical tips to ensure you stick to your new lifestyle.

Of course, the heart (pun intended) of this book is its recipes. Starting with chapter two, you will be introduced to an array of delightful and wholesome recipes, covering every meal of the day and every craving you might have. From vibrant smoothies, breakfast bowls, and teas, to seafood dishes packed with omega-3s, and hearty poultry and meat recipes, you'll have a plethora of options to choose from. Not to forget, this book also considers dietary preferences and restrictions with an entire chapter dedicated to plant-based dishes.

For our carb enthusiasts, there's a special section that

features healthful potatoes, pasta, and grains. These are meals that are sure to leave you satiated without the guilt of indulging. The soup and stew section includes recipes that are perfect for a cozy dinner or a hearty lunch. And, because we understand that a meal feels incomplete without something sweet at the end, a dessert section is added with a variety of delectable and guilt-free recipes.

The last chapter of the book is focused on sauces and dressings. These homemade accompaniments can elevate any meal, adding an extra burst of flavor to your dishes. Each sauce and dressing is made keeping in mind the principles of a low-cholesterol diet. You can trust that every recipe in this book has been carefully developed and tested to ensure it fits within the guidelines of a heart-healthy lifestyle.

The concluding pages of the book include a series of references to trusted organizations that provide additional information on cholesterol, heart disease, and dietary guidelines. You'll also find a handy measurement conversions chart to aid in your cooking endeavors.

"The Fast and Healthy Low Cholesterol Cookbook" is designed to be more than just a cookbook. It is a guide that will walk with you on your journey to better health. It aims to empower you, the reader, with the knowledge and tools necessary to take control of your health, while offering a broad range of delectable dishes that put a premium on taste and enjoyment, alongside health and nutrition.

Whether you're an expert cook or a beginner, this book is intended to make the kitchen a welcoming, accessible place. From the simple to the more complex, the recipes herein cater to a range of skill levels, and there is ample advice on how to make these meals as stress-free and enjoyable as possible. The aim is to make the act of cooking less of a chore and more of a rewarding experience.

What sets this cookbook apart is its dedication to not just the how, but also the why of low-cholesterol cooking. As such, it's as much an educational resource as it is a recipe collection. Through this book, you will gain a deeper understanding of cholesterol, its role in your body, and how the foods you consume can directly affect your health. But beyond theory, the book will also guide you in implementing these principles into your daily life through practical tips, diet guidelines, and of course, our carefully curated recipes.

One of the challenges of maintaining a low-cholesterol diet is finding variety and flavor in the foods we eat. This is why our chapters are organized to cover a broad spectrum of meals and cuisines, ensuring there's something for everyone. From a quick weekday breakfast to a leisurely weekend dinner, from an intimate meal for two to a feast for the whole family, this book has got you covered.

For those who are cautious about their protein intake, chapters dedicated to fish and seafood, poultry, beef and pork are included. Yet, those who prefer plant-based dishes are equally catered for with an entire chapter dedicated to vegan and vegetarian meals. Pasta, grains, and potato lovers will find a wealth of dishes to savor. For those chilly evenings or when you need a comforting meal, a selection of soups and stews is at your disposal.

The cherry on top is our dessert section. Who said a low-cholesterol diet means bidding adieu to sweets? From fresh fruit compotes to dark chocolate treats, these desserts will satisfy your sweet tooth without wreaking havoc on your cholesterol levels.

Moreover, the chapter on sauces and dressings will equip you with a repertoire of flavor boosters. These accompaniments are often overlooked in cookbooks but can elevate any dish from good to great. Homemade and free from preservatives, they not only taste better but are also better for your health.

"The Fast and Healthy Low Cholesterol Cookbook" acknowledges that taking steps towards a healthier lifestyle can be daunting, particularly when changes to diet are involved. However, this book aims to demonstrate that this journey need not be restrictive or boring. Instead, it can be an exciting exploration of flavors, textures, and cuisines, all within the parameters of a heart-healthy diet.

Whether you're a seasoned cook seeking new inspiration or a novice looking for guidance, whether you're embarking on a low-cholesterol diet out of necessity or choice, this book is your companion. It is designed to make the transition less overwhelming, more enjoyable, and absolutely delicious.

Here's to a journey of flavorful discoveries, healthier choices, and a more heart-friendly lifestyle. It's time to get cooking!

CONTENTS

.

Chapter Two: Smoothies, Beverages, and Breakfasts

Getting Started

A high-cholesterol diagnosis does not mean you have to give up all the foods you love or spend hours in the kitchen cooking new dishes.

Yes, you will need to adopt a new approach to diet and exercise. That alone can feel intimidating at first—I know it was for me. But you can shift to a heart-healthy diet and exercise plan without it consuming every minute of your day.

I was first diagnosed with high cholesterol in 2010. Reluctant to immediately jump to a statin medication, my doctor and I agreed on a plan to lower my cholesterol naturally with diet and exercise. We made an appointment to re-check my cholesterol in six months and she handed me a copy of the DASH (Dietary Approaches to Stop Hypertension) diet. I considered myself a fairly healthy eater at the time, so I was shocked to find that the DASH diet felt like a drastic change. Not only that, I didn't understand why my doctor had recommended a diet designed to lower blood pressure when I needed a *cholesterol-lowering* diet and exercise plan.

Turns out, several well-known diets (DASH, Mediterranean) meet the nutritional guidelines for lowering cholesterol. They accomplish this by limiting saturated and trans fats, and emphasizing fruits, vegetables, whole grains, nuts, fiber, and low-fat proteins like fish and poultry. The fact that multiple popular diets can work to lower cholesterol is great in theory. But in practice, having to choose between several diet programs or figure out how to mix and match recipes can feel overwhelming.

I knew I had to act—my doctor was very clear that my blood test results put me at increased risk for heart disease. She also stressed how important it is to treat high cholesterol early to avoid plaque buildup in the arteries, which can lead to a stroke and/or heart attack. Put simply, plaque can cause clots that block blood flow to the brain (stroke) or heart (heart attack). I knew I needed a plan, but the DASH diet itself didn't feel cholesterol-specific enough for my new lifestyle.

So, I began my own research. How could I implement a heart-healthy lifestyle and adjust my diet and exercise plan without it taking over my life? How could I eat healthier without it requiring a huge amount of time and effort—and without sacrificing flavor? Could I still have wine, ice cream, and chocolate?

To document what I learned about how to lower cholesterol through diet and exercise, and to capture recipes that were easy, delicious, and heart-healthy, I started the *Going Lo-Co* blog in 2011. Then in 2018, I wrote *The Low Cholesterol Cookbook and Action Plan*, with in-depth information about cholesterol and an action plan for adopting a heart-healthy lifestyle. And now, with *The 30-Minute Low-Cholesterol Cookbook*, I'm excited to share cholesterol information along with quick-and-easy recipes that make heart-healthy meals achievable—even on a busy weeknight.

Of course, changing habits is never easy. You will need to change what you eat. True, you will need to limit (or cut out) red meat and full-fat dairy and other foods high in saturated fat. True, you will need to watch and limit your sodium and sugar intake. And you will need to exercise daily. But exercising can be as easy as walking briskly for just 30 minutes a day, and a heart-healthy diet is truly not that hard to implement with the right support. Best of all, it can work: I was lifted out of the "needs a statin" group after just six months of slightly more exercise along with adding cholesterol-lowering foods and swapping red meat for lower fat proteins. In nine years of living what I call a "lo-co" lifestyle, my cholesterol levels have stayed at an acceptable level. (And a bit of wine and chocolate are still featured in my daily diet!)

It's a change that can benefit everyone—from those already managing heart disease and taking a statin medication to those of us striving to lower cholesterol naturally. Choosing a cholesterol-lowering approach to food and exercise can reduce your risk of heart disease.

Taking control and making a shift to a heart-healthy lifestyle can be empowering. Not only that, but it's exciting to discover healthy alternatives to your favorite foods, and find new, healthy, 30-minute recipes that are packed with flavor.

Let's get cooking!

CHAPTER ONE

The Cholesterol-Diet Connection

A dopting a heart-healthy, cholesterol-lowering lifestyle is a shift that can benefit anyone diagnosed with high cholesterol. Not enough exercise and eating the wrong kinds of food often contribute to high cholesterol. But that also means that a lifestyle that incorporates exercise and eating heart-healthy foods can help naturally lower cholesterol.

This chapter will cover the basics of cholesterol: what it is and how it works in the body. I'll explain which foods are scientifically known to reduce cholesterol. And I'll present tools that can help make it easier to launch your cholesterol-lowering lifestyle.

What Is Cholesterol?

Cholesterol is a waxy, fat-like substance naturally produced by our bodies to help build cells. While it is technically not a fat, cholesterol is encased in lipids (fats) that enable it to travel through the bloodstream. The problem is not cholesterol alone—everyone has it, and we naturally produce all we need. The issue is that the standard American diet (SAD) contains too much saturated fat, which causes our livers to produce an overabundance of cholesterol.

So if you have been diagnosed with a cholesterol problem, it's important to know which kind of cholesterol issue you have. There are three types of cholesterol, each with its own role and "target" that's considered healthy.

- LDL stands for low-density lipoproteins. The reason LDL cholesterol is often referred to as the "bad" cholesterol is because too much LDL cholesterol can cause plaque to build on the artery walls. The more LDL cholesterol in the blood, the greater the risk of heart disease.

- HDL stands for high-density lipoproteins. HDL cholesterol is known as the "good" cholesterol because it moves cholesterol to the liver, which eliminates it from the body. A higher HDL cholesterol level is desirable; a low count of HDL cholesterol increases the risk of heart disease.

- Triglycerides are a type of fat found in blood. High triglycerides increase heart disease risk, especially among women.

Lowering LDL cholesterol that is too high is important. When a person has excess cholesterol, it can accumulate and stick to the walls of the arteries as plaque. Thick, hard plaque can then narrow the arteries and make them less flexible; this dangerous condition is known as atherosclerosis (hardening of the arteries). If a blood clot forms and encounters an artery narrowed by plaque, the result can be a heart attack and/or a stroke.

Your risk of developing high cholesterol depends on several aspects of your lifestyle you can control, such as:

- Following a heart-healthy diet
- Exercising at least 30 minutes daily
- Not smoking
- Having a desired body fat percentage

It also depends on factors out of your control, such as genetics, medical conditions, your age, sex, and ethnicity.

If you have noncontrollable risk factors, monitoring your cholesterol is vital. For example, since medical conditions such as diabetes and high blood pressure elevate heart disease risk, undiagnosed high cholesterol might further increase that risk. And everyone's cholesterol increases with age: The risk of high cholesterol increases when men reach age 45 and women reach age 55. There are also sex differences: Premenopausal women tend to have lower LDL cholesterol than men, and men often have lower HDL cholesterol than women.

High cholesterol can run in families. You may be at increased risk of high cholesterol if early heart disease affected your father or brother (before age 55) or mother or sister (before age 65).

As for ethnicity, the American Heart Association (AHA) reports that cholesterol levels vary by race and ethnicity, with higher levels of LDL cholesterol seen most often among Hispanic/Latino men and white women. Further, the 2018 *Guideline on the Management of Blood Cholesterol* report explains race/ethnicity factors can influence heart disease risk, including: "those who identify as South Asians . . . those who identify as East Asians, and the increased prevalence of hypertension in blacks and African Americans."

Doctors decide whether to treat high cholesterol with medication based on a calculation of a person's 10-year risk of heart disease—cholesterol is one key input—along with an assessment of the lifestyle and noncontrollable factors listed above. Interestingly, the heart disease risk calculator doctors use is available to everyone! If you are over 40 and are not already taking a statin and have not been diagnosed with heart disease, to calculate your own personal 10-year risk of heart disease, all you need are your blood pressure and cholesterol test results. A link to the easy, online Atherosclerotic Cardiovascular Disease (ASCVD) Risk Calculator is included in the Resources section at the back of this book. It takes just minutes to complete, and you can—and should—discuss your results with your doctor.

If your risk of heart disease is high, your doctor may prescribe cholesterol-lowering medication (although eliminating cholesterol is never the goal—your body needs some, just not too much. In fact, too little might be linked with depression). If you smoke or are overweight, your doctor will work with you to reduce those risk factors. Almost certainly, they will advocate for a regular exercise plan and heart-healthy diet.

By picking up this book you've already started on the path to lowering your cholesterol naturally, with a heart-healthy diet. Let's jump on in and examine how making the right food choices can help reduce your cholesterol.

A Closer Look at Cholesterol Levels

Cholesterol is no longer managed to a set, specific target level. Rather the decision to treat high cholesterol with medication is based on cholesterol blood test results along with an assessment of personal risk. This personal risk is evaluated using both the ASCVD Risk Calculator (which estimates a person's 10-year risk of heart disease) as well as an assessment of heart disease risk factors beyond high cholesterol and high blood pressure, such as: age, sex, heredity, history of diabetes, tobacco use, alcohol use, exercise level, and weight.

However, there are general guidelines for what constitutes healthy cholesterol levels:

- For triglycerides, a level below 150 mg/dL* is considered normal.

- While not used as treatment targets, the National Heart, Lung, and Blood Institute website summarizes the following as healthy blood cholesterol levels:**

Age/Sex	Total Cholesterol	LDL	HDL
Age 19 or younger	Less than 170 mg/dL	Less than 100 mg/dL	More than 45 mg/dL
Men age 20 or	125 to 200	Less than 100	40 mg/dL or

older	mg/dL	mg/dL	higher
Women age 20 or older	125 to 200 mg/dL	Less than 100 mg/dL	50 mg/dL or higher

*Cholesterol is measured as milligrams (mg) per deciliter (dL) of blood.
**Chart and triglyceride source: Diagnosis tab of
www.nhlbi.nih.gov/health-topics/high-blood-cholesterol.

Low-Cholesterol Eating Principles

Making a change doesn't have to be all or nothing. If it doesn't feel reasonable to you to completely shift how you eat overnight, that's okay. You can start by slowly working in the principles of a heart-healthy diet, and making gradual changes until it becomes your new "normal" pattern of eating.

Here's what you need to know:

- **The most important place to start is to limit your intake of saturated fat.** According to the AHA, the best way to lower your cholesterol is to reduce saturated fat and trans fat intake. Specifically, saturated fats should be limited to 5 to 6 percent of daily calories (see Diet Guidelines section) and trans fats should be avoided entirely.

- **Then choose meals centered on heart-healthy fruits and vegetables, lean proteins, and heart-healthy oils.** Every five years, the United States Departments of Health and Human Services (HHS) and of Agriculture (USDA) jointly publish a report with nutritional and dietary information and guidelines. the *Dietary Guidelines for Americans 2015–2020* describes a heart-healthy diet as an eating pattern that is comprised of vegetables, fruits, whole grains, legumes, and nuts. It includes low-fat dairy products and lean proteins such as poultry and fish (high in omega-3 fatty acids)—and avoids red meat, full-fat dairy, and processed foods. For cooking, nontropical vegetable oils (such as olive or canola oils instead of coconut or palm oils) are recommended, as is limiting sodium, sweets and desserts, and sugar-sweetened beverages.

- **Dietary fiber is key to lowering cholesterol.** There are two forms of dietary fiber: soluble and insoluble. While both are important for digestive health, soluble fiber helps reduce cholesterol. Derived from plants, soluble fiber slows digestion and attaches to cholesterol as it moves through and out of your body. As The National Lipid Association explains: "Eating 5 to 10 grams of soluble fiber a day can help lower total and LDL cholesterol by 5 to 11 points, and sometimes more." In terms of total dietary fiber, the Food and Drug Administration specifies 25 grams per day for a 2,000-calorie diet. And while there is no dietary reference intake for insoluble or soluble fiber, many experts recommend a total dietary fiber intake of 25 to 30 grams per day with about one-fourth (6 to 8 grams per day) coming from soluble fiber. Dietary soluble fiber is found in oat bran, barley, nuts, seeds, beans, lentils, peas, and many fruits and vegetables. Specific sources include: beans (particularly black beans, lima beans, and kidney beans), oats/oatmeal, avocado, Brussels sprouts, broccoli, eggplant, okra, carrots, sweet potatoes (with skin), bananas, apples, grapes, strawberries, blueberries, figs, nectarines, apricots.

- **Add cholesterol-lowering foods.** These foods have been shown to help reduce cholesterol:

- Fish high in omega-3 fatty acids
- Foods fortified with phytosterols (see <u>Supplements</u>)
- Nuts
- Soy
- Vegetable oils

So how do you incorporate all this into an easy-to-follow, delicious diet? You might have heard that there are several diets often recommended for heart health:

- The DASH diet is designed to lower blood pressure by limiting sodium; it is also frequently recommended for lowering cholesterol.

- The Mediterranean diet follows the low-cholesterol principles previously outlined. It is low in saturated fat and focused on vegetables, fruits, and olive oil, making it beneficial for cardiovascular health.

- The Therapeutic Lifestyle Changes (TLC) diet also follows the low-cholesterol principles. In the TLC diet, 25 to 35 percent of daily calories are from fat (mainly unsaturated), saturated fat comprises less than 7 percent of daily calories, trans fats are avoided, and it specifies consuming no more than 200 mg of dietary cholesterol per day.

Much like these diet programs, the recipes in this book adhere to the most important principles of a cholesterol-lowering eating plan: They are low in saturated fat and are built around heart-healthy fruits and vegetables. Some are high in fiber. Some include omega-3 fatty fish. Some are lean-protein or soy-based. Since all the recipes in this book are designed to help lower cholesterol, you can easily start incorporating heart-healthy eating into your daily life by selecting the recipes that appeal to you most, and adding them to your weekly meal plan.

30 Minutes to Heart-Healthy Eating

This book was designed with one key goal: to make it fast and easy to eat in a heart-healthy way. Each flavorful recipe can be made in 30 minutes, uses familiar ingredients, and employs everyday cooking techniques. We've covered breakfast, lunch, dinner, and even dressings and dessert. So, all you have to do to kick-start an eating plan that can help lower cholesterol naturally is choose recipes.

These delicious recipes make it easy to comply. With minimal prep and cook times (some recipes involve no cooking whatsoever) you'll be eating low-cholesterol meals in a matter of minutes. And for the most part, the recipes don't require special kitchen equipment or foreign ingredients that are expensive or difficult to procure.

That said, the reality is that changing your eating habits is not like flipping a switch. Every meal presents an opportunity to make a choice: the old way of eating or the new, heart-healthy style. The wide range of recipes in this book support you in making healthy choices daily. What's challenging is the many opportunities you are faced with all day to revert to familiar, unhealthy ways of eating.

Some days—hopefully most days—you'll be able to make a heart-healthy choice at every meal. But sometimes you'll falter. We all do. What's important is not that unhealthy choice; it's what you choose next. One "bad" meal choice doesn't have to ruin your heart-healthy goals for the entire day.

Did you have fried food at lunch? Instead of feeling like you failed, look at it as an opportunity to reframe the rest of your day with low saturated fat choices. Maybe you can add a handful of cholesterol-lowering nuts for your afternoon snack and plan for a healthy fish dinner.

If you know, on a particular day, that a heart-healthy meal is going to be hard or impossible to access—maybe if it's simply going to be a burger kind of day—just make the best choices you can within that framework. Choose chicken or a single-patty hamburger instead of a double-patty cheeseburger. Pat yourself on the back for *not* ordering a sugary drink. What's key to making a heart-healthy lifestyle stick is doing what you can every day, at every meal, to make your choices as heart-healthy as possible.

Choosing recipes from this book rather than preparing meals featuring old standbys like red meat, bacon, and options heavy on the cheese is an important step on your heart-healthy path. You're not going to be perfect in your daily choices, and that is okay. The goal is to make heart-healthy choices as often as you can, until one day you realize you have a new, heart-healthy way of eating all the time.

You'll know you are well on your way when choosing the foods that are known to reduce LDL cholesterol becomes a habit. Our hope is that many of our 30-minute, easy-to-make heart-healthy, delicious recipes, become weeknight staples in your household.

Diet Guidelines

There are four major food culprits that raise LDL cholesterol: saturated fats, trans fats, salt, and food with added sugars. The recipes in this book limit exposure to these harmful substances by replacing them with heart-healthy ingredients assembled into flavorful recipes that take only 30 minutes to prepare.

What to eat:

- Choose lean proteins such as fish and poultry without skin. (If you choose to eat meat, look for the leanest cuts available and prepare healthily, without added saturated fats and sodium.)

- Eat fish at least twice a week, especially fish high in omega-3 fatty acids, such as salmon.
- Choose low-fat dairy products.
- Eat an abundance of colorful fruits and vegetables.
- Incorporate whole grains.
- Reach for fiber-rich foods such as oat bran, beans, seeds, and nuts.
- Choose cholesterol-lowering foods (see here).
- Cook with monounsaturated and polyunsaturated oils, such as olive or canola oil, instead of butter or tropical oils, such as coconut or palm oil.

What not to eat (or what to limit):

- Limit saturated fat to no more than 5 to 6 percent of total daily calories; that's 13 grams of saturated fat for a 2,000-calorie-per-day diet (see chart below).
- Avoid trans fats entirely (avoid food made with partially hydrogenated oil).
- Reduce sodium to no more than 2,300 mg per day (1,500 mg if you have high blood pressure).
- Avoid refined or added sugars and refined grains.

Saturated Fat and Trans Fats

As limiting saturated fat (and avoiding trans fats) is critical to a heart-healthy diet—and probably where habits need most adjusting—here's a guide published by the National Heart, Lung, and Blood Institute (NHLBI). It provides a recommendation for the maximum amount of saturated fat that should be eaten per day when following a diet aimed at reducing cholesterol:

If You Consume: Calories Per Day	Eat No More Than: Saturated Fat (6%)
1,200	8 grams
1,500	10 grams
1,800	12 grams
2,000	13 grams
2,500	17 grams

That means that for those following a typical 2,000-calorie per day diet, no more than 13 grams of saturated fat should be consumed in an entire day (for example, a McDonald's Big Mac is loaded with 33 grams of fat and of that, 8 grams are saturated fat).

Specifically, here's how you can limit saturated fat and avoid trans fats:

- **Limit saturated fat to no more than 5 to 6 percent of total daily calories** (13 grams of saturated fat for a 2,000-calorie-a-day diet). Do this by severely limiting—or better, avoiding—red meats, deli and processed meats, full-fat dairy, butter, and/or tropical oils. Instead, choose lean meats, poultry without skin, skim milk, and cook with olive oil and/or canola oil.

- **Avoid trans fats entirely.** Trans fats (primarily found in partially hydrogenated oils, or PHOs) are so unhealthy they are considered unsafe. They lurk in baked goods and processed foods such as cookies, crackers, cakes, stick margarine, coffee creamers, refrigerated dough, and ready-to-use frosting, as well as in frozen foods and fried fast food.

If your current diet is loaded with saturated fat, transitioning to a heart-healthy diet that limits saturated fat offers a great opportunity to lower your cholesterol. You don't have to give up all your favorite foods. Being more mindful of your food choices and opting for healthier, low-fat options is a great way to start improving your heart health. The delectable, heart-healthy recipes in this book can help get you going.

Recommended Daily Dietary Cholesterol

For many years, eggs were considered unhealthy because they are high in dietary cholesterol (one large egg contains about 210 mg of dietary cholesterol, and the recommended daily limit was previously 300 mg per day.) That shifted with the *2015–2020 Dietary Guidelines for Americans,* when the USDA removed the daily dietary cholesterol limit and named eggs a healthy protein (but to be clear, the *Guidelines* still advised as little dietary cholesterol as possible). The reason for the removal of the specific dietary cholesterol limit was twofold. First, the focus in the *Guidelines* was on a "healthy eating pattern" which, by default, limits consumption of dietary cholesterol. It is now believed that consuming saturated fat, not dietary cholesterol, is the culprit in raising cholesterol and heart disease risk.

More studies will likely be done, and the USDA may update the *Dietary Guidelines for Americans.* It's probably safest to limit dietary cholesterol to 300 mg per day or 200 mg per day if you have a higher risk of heart disease.

Animal products contain dietary cholesterol, while vegetable, fruits, and most grains do not. Just one serving of these foods will put you over the daily target for dietary cholesterol: organ meats (chicken liver has 631 mg in a 3.5 ounce serving; beef liver has 389 mg), squid (231 mg), shrimp (200 mg), and eggs (1 egg has 212 mg).

Full-fat dairy has more dietary cholesterol than lower fat options: One cup of whole milk has 33 mg of dietary cholesterol, whereas skim milk delivers only 10 mg. Fish, chicken, and lean cuts of meat tend to have lower dietary cholesterol levels than beef: a 3.5-ounce serving of beef sirloin has 89 mg of dietary cholesterol versus 41 mg for halibut.

The Diet Connection

Diet is one part—a crucial part—to lowering cholesterol naturally. But managing high cholesterol requires a multipronged approach that includes additional "lo-co" lifestyle choices. Overall cholesterol-lowering lifestyle choices include: a diet based on heart-healthy foods, living smoke-free, achieving a healthy weight, and regular exercise. While the jury is out on several popular dietary supplements, there are many that can play a role in lowering cholesterol.

Supplements

Although it is always best to choose cholesterol-lowering and heart-healthy foods rather than supplements, a couple of nutritional supplements do help reduce cholesterol. Supplements that can be worth adding to a cholesterol-lowering diet include:

- **Foods with added phytosterols.** Plant sterols and stanol esters are naturally occurring substances in plants that help block the absorption of cholesterol. Such foods as margarine, orange juice, and cereals that have been fortified with added plant sterols can help reduce LDL cholesterol. Aim for 2 grams of phytosterols per day for cholesterol-lowering properties, but do not add extra calories or fats to get to that level. What's recommended is swapping out current consumption of spreads or juice for versions fortified with phytosterols.

- **Psyllium.** While fiber-rich foods should be part of your heart-healthy diet, it can be challenging to reach the AHA recommended 25 grams of dietary fiber per day (for a 2,000 calorie diet). That's why fiber supplements are popular among people seeking to lower their cholesterol. Psyllium is a soluble fiber derived from the seeds of the herb *Plantago ovata*. A daily dose of a psyllium fiber supplement (Metamucil, Citrucel, or FiberCon) delivers a reliable shot of cholesterol-reducing fiber.

Many believe there are other dietary supplements that can help lower cholesterol, but research does not fully support the use of those supplements. According to the National Center for Complementary and Integrative Health, "The dietary supplements red yeast rice, flaxseed, and garlic are among the many supplements that have been studied for lowering cholesterol levels. Unfortunately, there isn't conclusive evidence that any of these supplements are effective in reducing cholesterol levels."

Because the following supplements have not been studied enough or have not been proven effective at lowering cholesterol, they are *not* recommended:

- Artichoke leaf extract
- Buckwheat
- Fenugreek
- Garlic
- Grape polyphenols
- Guggul extract (guggulipid)
- Hawthorn fruit
- Policosanol
- Selenium
- Soy protein
- Tea catechins

Further, a warning about red yeast rice supplements. Some red yeast rice products contain a substance, monacolin K, that is chemically identical to lovastatin, a cholesterol-lowering statin drug, while some do not. It is not possible for a consumer to tell whether a red yeast rice product contains monacolin K, but if it does, the FDA has stated such products cannot be legally sold as a dietary supplement. That is because this chemical also affects the liver and thus, should only be taken under a doctor's supervision.

A note about fish oil supplements. While the omega-3 fatty acids found in fish *can* lower LDL cholesterol and triglycerides, fish oil supplements are currently not recommended to lower cholesterol for people not being treated for heart disease, according to an analysis of randomized clinical trials conducted by the AHA.

Exercise

For overall cardiovascular health, the AHA recommends everyone—not just those with high cholesterol—get 150 minutes per week of moderate-intensity exercise. That's 30 minutes a day, five days a week. And since brisk walking counts, this is an activity almost everyone can do!

Moderate-intensity activities include:

- Gardening
- Water aerobics
- Dancing
- Doubles tennis
- Brisk walking (at least 2.5 miles per hour)
- Biking (slower than 10 miles per hour)

If that type of exercise doesn't appeal to you, as an alternative, the AHA recommends at least 75 minutes of vigorous-intensity physical exercise throughout the week to lower cholesterol and improve cardiovascular health. In short, 25 minutes of a vigorous physical activity three days a week will improve heart health.

Vigorous-intensity exercise results in a sweat and includes such activities as:

- Running
- Swimming laps
- Tennis
- Aerobic dance
- Jumping rope
- Hiking uphill or hiking with a heavy backpack
- Spinning or cycling (10 miles per hour or faster)

The AHA also recommends moderate- to high-intensity muscle-strengthening activity (simple weight-bearing exercises such as resistance bands, machines, or free weights) at least two days per week.

If this level of exercise seems like a lot, you can start with walking and build up your endurance. Since even normal walking will result in progress and vigorous walking counts, you can get your cholesterol-lowering exercise minutes in without stepping foot in a gym or scheduling an exercise class. You might even be surprised at how quickly you progress, and are able to walk longer and/or more quickly. And of course, it's always important to talk with your doctor before beginning any kind of exercise regimen.

The Low-Cholesterol Kitchen: Tips for Easier Home Cooking

Naturally lowering your cholesterol is not a fad diet. To be successful, you need to embrace a heart-healthy lifestyle. Our goal is to make it as easy as possible for you to go heart-healthy.

Starting your journey is as easy as choosing and preparing recipes from this book. We've included breakfast, lunch, dinner, and even dessert, so your day is fully covered. All the delicious recipes are heart-healthy, and can be prepared in 30 minutes or less.

There is no need to vigilantly count calories (unless you like to!), there are no special cooking techniques, and the only special ingredients you'll need are fresh fruits and vegetables and heart-healthy grains and proteins.

There are a few hacks that make it easier to prepare heart-healthy meals every day. It all starts with making sure your kitchen, pantry, and refrigerator are stocked for success. Let's launch your new low-cholesterol lifestyle.

The Low-Cholesterol Pantry, Spice Rack, Refrigerator, and Freezer

A change to a heart-healthy cooking style will be easier to adopt and stick with if you have the right ingredients on hand—and if you limit your access to former unhealthy ingredients.

Donate or Toss

Start by ridding your kitchen of ingredients that have no place in your new heart-healthy lifestyle.

- **Proteins high in saturated fat.** These include red meat, cured meats like hot dogs, bacon and sausage, and deli meats. You'll be replacing these with lean proteins such as fish and poultry without skin.

- **Unhealthy Oils.** Any margarine that contains trans fat, all tropical oils (coconut and palm oil), all partially hydrogenated vegetable oils, and any oil or fat that is solid at room temperature. You will replace these with heart-healthy monounsaturated oils like olive and canola. If you use a "butter" spread, choose one fortified with phytosterols. (NOTE: If your refrigerator simply must contain butter—for other household members, for example—keep it out of sight so it does not tempt. If absolutely necessary, you can use butter sparingly in recipes, but never as a spread.)

- **High-fat dairy products.** These include ice cream, full-fat whole milk, cream, full-fat cheese and yogurt, and sour cream. You'll be opting instead for fat-free (skim) or 1% milk and dairy products, and/or soy and plant-based dairy. You will notice that some of the recipes in this book do contain full-fat yogurt—this is because lower-fat yogurts tend to be loaded with sugar. Rest assured, all of the recipes in this book adhere to our cholesterol guidelines.

- **Refined grains.** White rice and pasta have no place in your new pantry. You'll replace these with whole-grain varieties.

Top Pantry Staples

If you keep your kitchen stocked with the common heart-healthy ingredients used in this book, shopping for a particular recipe could be as easy as zipping through the refrigerated and fresh produce aisles. Having these items on hand will make it easier to prepare the heart-healthy meals in this book:

- A variety of no-salt nuts, especially almonds and walnuts

- Brown rice
- Bulgur
- Canned and boxed low-sodium broths
- Canned no-salt-added tomato products, such as paste, diced tomatoes, and sauce
- Dried peas
- Extra-virgin olive oil
- Lentils
- Low-sodium soy or tamari sauce
- Oatmeal: rolled or steel-cut oats
- Pearled barley
- Quinoa
- Sesame oil
- Wheat bran and oat-based cereals
- Whole-grain pasta

About Quinoa

"Prewashed" quinoa is not washed; instead, the outer layer has been scraped off, which removes nutrients. I recommend purchasing quinoa unwashed; it's not difficult to wash it yourself. It must be washed to remove the natural soapy saponins, which can create stomach upset in many people.

Staple Herbs and Spices

- Black and white pepper
- Chili powder

- Curry powder
- Dried oregano leaves
- Dried thyme leaves
- Fresh basil leaves (it's easy to grow basil in pots on your windowsill)
- Fresh flat-leaf parsley
- Ground cinnamon
- Ground ginger
- Ground turmeric

Top Staple Refrigerated Items

- Plant-based and low-fat dairy milk
- Hot sauces
- Large eggs
- Lemons
- Low-fat Greek style yogurt
- Low-sodium mustard
- Nonfat sour cream
- Tofu and tempeh

Top Staple Freezer Items

- 98% lean ground beef
- Boneless skinless chicken breasts
- Fish fillets (such as salmon, red snapper, cod)
- Fruits (bananas and berries with no sugar added)

- Ground turkey
- Pork tenderloin
- Soybeans (edamame)
- Vegetables (plain, without sauce)

Cholesterol Fighters

The most important element in eating to achieve lower cholesterol is to limit saturated fats and avoid trans fats. Instead, fill your plate with whole grains and an array of colorful fruits and vegetables. And there are specific ingredients that some studies have shown can help lower cholesterol, so add as many of these as possible:

- **Oatmeal, bran, and high-fiber foods.** To reach the cholesterol-lowering target of 25 grams per day of fiber, you'll want to ensure every meal and snack includes fiber-rich foods such as oats, bran, bananas, berries, nuts, whole grains, and even freshly popped popcorn.

- **Fish rich in omega-3 fatty acids.** Eating "fatty" fish two to three times a week delivers a healthier protein than red meat and provides triglyceride-reducing omega-3 fatty acids.

- **Avocados.** Packed with healthy monounsaturated fat (and other nutrients), using a creamy avocado—as a spread or layered onto a sandwich or chopped into a salad—instead of condiments loaded with saturated fat is a swap that will help lower cholesterol.

- **Nuts.** Multiple studies have demonstrated that eating about 2 ounces a day of almonds, walnuts, peanuts, and other nuts can lower LDL cholesterol. Unsalted is best.

- **Apples, grapes, strawberries, and citrus fruit.** Rich in pectin (when the skin is consumed) the soluble fiber in these fruits can help lower LDL cholesterol.

- **Dark chocolate.** Crave a little bit of sweet? Reach for 1 ounce of dark chocolate instead of a treat that's packed with saturated fat or baked goods with extremely unhealthy trans fats. The flavanols in dark chocolate have antioxidant properties that can help reduce cholesterol.

Stick-with-It Tips

Diets are notoriously hard to commit to, but a lifestyle change is different. Instead of a diet, where the focus is often on counting calories, shifting to a heart-healthy lifestyle is all about an attitude change. One key to success is feeling great about the choices you're now making. When you start to embrace cooking with a broad array of whole, heart-healthy foods, you'll be less likely to crave the unhealthy foods you used to eat.

If you stick to eating and cooking delicious, heart-healthy recipes, you'll be well on your way to lowering your cholesterol levels without counting a single calorie. We've made it easy for you by providing 125 recipes that taste great and can be on the table in 30 minutes or less.

Beyond quick recipes, here are some of the kitchen tricks I routinely use to make heart-healthy cooking easier to plan, prep, and stick to:

- **Create a meal plan.** You're less likely to order out when you've planned and shopped for your weekly, heart-healthy meals.

- **Batch cook.** Roasting fresh vegetables over the weekend sets you up for the week.

- **Double up recipes and freeze.** Double up and freeze recipe favorites for those inevitable nights you just don't feel like cooking. To avoid freezer burn or defrosting an unintended meal, don't forget to label with the recipe name and date!

- **Buy prediced fresh onions.** No tears. No excess water when thawed.

- **Buy zucchini noodles to add to pasta.** A quick sauté in olive oil and garlic and your pasta gets an invisible veggie boost. Picky eaters may not even notice!

- **Buy fresh, peeled garlic cloves and use a garlic press.** If you like garlic, this no-peel option delivers fresh flavor in seconds.

- **Use ginger paste instead of fresh ginger.** Heart-healthy ginger is hard to peel. For those who don't mind giving up a bit of flavor for a lot of ease, I recommend jarred ginger paste.

- **Keep "Emergency Chicken" in the freezer.** Individually wrapped chicken breasts are great for those weeks you don't have time to meal plan or when your mood shifts.

- **Keep green sauce and mustard vinaigrette in the refrigerator to use on fish, chicken, and salad.** Heart-healthy sauces dress a salad or add zip to bland proteins with just a shake of the bottle.

- **Stay stocked up.** Use a shareable, app-based shopping list (I like the free app, *AnyList*) to instantly and easily add a key pantry item the moment it runs low.

Eating Out with High Cholesterol

Your heart-healthy lifestyle doesn't have to grind to a halt when you're out to eat. There are two key areas to consider when dining out: saturated fat and sodium. Because restaurant food can be astonishingly high in salt—one meal can hit the daily limit of sodium—it's always best to ask for a low-salt preparation.

Start by scanning the menu for options low in saturated fat, with ingredients similar to your home cooking. Choose items made with lean proteins, whole grains, lots of fruits and vegetables, and heart-healthy fats. Here are some tips for selecting more heart-healthy menu items:

- Choose seafood or skinless poultry, and select preparations with little oil. Baked, grilled, steamed, broiled, and poached are all healthier than sautéed or fried.

- Order dressings and/or sauces on the side. For still-amazing taste with less fat, dip your fork into the dressing first and then spear your salad or protein. You might be surprised at the flavor punch delivered by just a small amount of dressing or sauce.

- Customize your meal. Ask for your protein grilled instead of fried, for a baked potato instead of fries, and to double the vegetables.

- Stay away from dishes with high-fat descriptions such as: creamy, au gratin, au fromage, breaded, fried, stuffed, or scalloped. Avoid butter or cheese sauces.

- Sip water or seltzer throughout your meal. You'll feel full faster, which helps prevent overeating.

- Bypass high-fat desserts (or have just a bite). Instead, select fruit or sorbet. Or, skip dessert altogether and indulge in a low-fat treat at home.

ORDERING BY CUISINE

The overall guidelines can be used at any restaurant. While you'll of course want to check the specific restaurant's fat content and preparation style, here are some ordering tips by cuisine:

- **Chinese:** Eat this: moo shu vegetables, moo shu chicken, moo goo gai pan, Chinese eggplant with garlic sauce, chicken and broccoli, Buddha's delight, chicken lettuce wraps, steamed vegetable dumplings. For all, ask your server for the kitchen to go light on the sauce. Avoid fried dumplings (fried anything) and beef/red meat dishes.

- **Japanese:** Eat this: miso soup, edamame, sashimi, sushi (particularly salmon, tuna, veggie, California and rainbow rolls). Ask for low-sodium soy sauce. Avoid tempura, katsu, and sushi (or any dish) made with mayonnaise.

- **Italian:** Eat this: thin crust pizza with vegetable toppings (not meat), and ask to go easy on the cheese, pasta fagioli, pasta primavera.

Avoid pizza with meat or extra cheese, pasta with cream sauce, chicken parmigiana, lasagna, risotto.

- **Mexican:** Eat this: gazpacho, black bean soup, fajitas, chicken or seafood tacos (but skip the sour cream and go light on the cheese). Avoid this: corn chips, nachos, chili con carne, creamy soups, refried beans, chimichangas, anything fried.

- **Indian:** Eat this: dal, tandoori chicken, tandoori fish, chana masala, aloo gobi, kebabs. Avoid this: pappadam, naan, pakoras, samosas, saag paneer, chicken tikka masala, lamb rogan josh, navratan korma.

About the Recipes

These recipes were developed to be low in saturated fat, dietary cholesterol, sodium, and sugar, and high in vitamins, minerals, fiber, healthy fat—and taste! Whole foods are used in the recipes to get the most nutrition out of every bite. If you use whole foods instead of processed foods, your health will naturally improve.

Aside from being heart-healthy, another great thing about these recipes is that you will not feel deprived. Whole vegetables, fruits, grains, and lean meats are full of flavor in and of themselves.

Each recipe should only take 30 minutes to prepare and cook, which we were able to achieve by limiting the steps. And every ingredient is easy to find—either in the grocery store or online.

The recipes are labeled: "Vegan," "Vegetarian," "Pescatarian," "Gluten-Free," and "Nut-Free." When an ingredient that can cause allergic reactions is used, we often give you options in a recipe tip.

Begin experimenting with these recipes and you'll be well on your way to establishing your heart-healthy way of life!

Baked French Toast Strips with Mixed Berry Sauce

CHAPTER TWO

Smoothies, Beverages, and Breakfasts

Pineapple Mixed Berry Smoothie

Matcha Green Tea and Peach Smoothie

Herbed Peach Tea

Ginger Pomegranate Sweet Tea

Orange Apricot Muesli

Cranberry Orange Mixed Grain Granola

Blueberry Almond Breakfast Bowl

Amaranth and Date Porridge

Curried Farro Hot Cereal

Spicy Omelet

Scrambled Egg Tacos

Asparagus Kale Frittata

Nutty Quinoa Waffles

Cinnamon Oat Bran Banana Pancakes

Baked French Toast Strips with Mixed Berry Sauce

Pineapple Mixed Berry Smoothie

VEGAN, GLUTEN-FREE, NUT-FREE

SERVES 2 / **PREP TIME:** 15 minutes

This delicious, thick and sweet smoothie has the most striking pink color. You can use any combination of berries you'd like in this recipe. They are all chock-full of fiber, vitamins, and flavor.

1 cup sliced strawberries
½ cup raspberries
½ cup cubed pineapple
½ cup low-fat soy milk
1 tablespoon fresh lemon juice
1 scoop protein powder
1 cup ice cubes

1. In a blender or food processor, combine the strawberries, raspberries, pineapple, soy milk, lemon juice, and protein powder.

2. Cover and blend until almost smooth.

3. Add the ice, cover, and blend until the mixture is thick and smooth. Pour into 2 tall glasses. Serve immediately.

COOKING TIP: If you make a lot of smoothies, you may want to invest in a good quality blender: one with a strong motor. Many ingredients used in smoothies contain a lot of fiber that resists blending. When the ingredients are fully blended, the flavor really pops.

Per serving: Calories 138; Fat 2g (with 11% calories from fat); Saturated fat 0g; Monounsaturated fat 0g; Carbs 21g; Sodium 163mg; Dietary fiber 5g; Protein 14g; Cholesterol 0mg; Vitamin A 3% DV; Vitamin C 115% DV; Sugar 12g

Matcha Green Tea and Peach Smoothie

VEGAN, GLUTEN-FREE, NUT-FREE

SERVES 2 / **PREP TIME:** 10 minutes

Smoothies are breakfast in a glass! This filling recipe features spinach for fiber, and peaches and bananas for their sweet and creamy qualities. Matcha is green tea that is ground so it blends easily with other ingredients.

1½ cups frozen peach slices
1 banana, peeled and sliced
¼ cup packed baby spinach leaves
¼ cup orange juice
1 tablespoon matcha green tea powder
2 tablespoons protein powder
1 teaspoon vanilla

1. In a blender or food processor, add the peaches, banana, spinach, orange juice, matcha, protein powder, and vanilla.

2. Cover and process on high until the mixture is smooth. Pour into two tall glasses. Serve immediately.

INGREDIENT TIP: When you add protein powder to breakfast smoothies it not only improves the consistency; it helps you feel full longer. You can find many different flavors and varieties of protein powder in most supermarkets as well as online. A good vegan brand is Naked Nutrition Pea Protein Isolate.

Per serving: Calories 161; Fat 1g (with 6% calories from fat); Saturated fat 0g; Monounsaturated fat 0g; Carbs 28g; Sodium 145mg; Dietary fiber 4g; Protein 14g; Cholesterol 0mg; Vitamin A 17% DV; Vitamin C 48% DV; Sugar 19g

Herbed Peach Tea

VEGAN, GLUTEN-FREE, NUT-FREE

SERVES 4 / **PREP TIME:** 15 minutes / **COOK TIME:** 4 minutes

Herbs such as basil and thyme have a slightly spicy, lemony flavor and aroma. They elegantly complement the sweet and tart flavor of peaches and the earthy taste of tea. Bonus: Basil also contains anti-inflammatory properties.

2 cups unsweetened peach nectar
1 bunch fresh basil leaves
1 sprig fresh thyme leaves
2 cups boiling water
2 bags green or white tea
1 tablespoon fresh lemon juice
Peach slices for garnish (optional)

1. Combine the peach nectar, basil, and thyme sprig in a medium saucepan. Using the back of a spoon, crush the herbs lightly to release their flavor. This is called muddling.

2. Add the water and bring to a simmer over medium heat. Reduce the heat to low, and simmer for 2 minutes.

3. Remove the pan from the heat and add the tea bags and lemon juice. Let steep for 2 minutes.

4. Strain the tea into a warmed teapot or glass serving container, and discard the tea bags and the herbs. Garnish with peach slices (if using). Serve immediately.

INGREDIENT TIP: Many peach nectars on the market contain added sugar. Make sure you check the label to see that it's just pure fruit juice.

Per serving: Calories 68; Fat 0g (with 0% calories from fat); Saturated fat 0g; Monounsaturated fat 0g; Carbs 18g; Sodium 9mg; Dietary fiber 1g; Protein 0g; Cholesterol 0mg; Vitamin A 6% DV; Vitamin C 14% DV; Sugar 17g

Ginger Pomegranate Sweet Tea

VEGETARIAN, GLUTEN-FREE, NUT-FREE

SERVES 4 / **PREP TIME:** 10 minutes / **COOK TIME:** 4 minutes

Pomegranates are an unusual fruit; you eat the juicy seeds (called arils) that are encased in a leathery shell. The fruit contains antioxidants that are anti-inflammatory, and also contains punicic acid, which can lower triglyceride levels in the blood.

2 cups unsweetened pomegranate juice
2 slices peeled ginger root, roughly chopped
2 cups water
2 bags herbal or green tea
1 tablespoon honey
1 tablespoon fresh lemon juice
½ teaspoon ground cinnamon

1. Combine the pomegranate juice, ginger root, and water in a medium nonreactive saucepan.

2. Bring the mixture to a simmer over medium heat. Reduce the heat to low and simmer for 2 minutes.

3. Remove the pan from the heat and add the tea bags. Let steep for 2 minutes. Stir in the honey, lemon juice and cinnamon.

4. Strain the mixture into a teapot or glass serving container, discarding the tea bags and solids. Serve immediately.

DID YOU KNOW? Pomegranate juice, like all fruit juices, has a lot of sugar. But in this fruit, the sugars are bound to antioxidants so the sugars are protective against atherosclerosis. Drinking pomegranate juice does not affect cholesterol levels, and it reduces the uptake of LDL cholesterol.

Per serving: Calories 85; Fat 0g (with 0% calories from fat); Saturated fat 0g; Monounsaturated fat 0g; Carbs 21g; Sodium 12mg; Dietary fiber 0g; Protein 0g; Cholesterol 0mg; Vitamin A 0% DV; Vitamin C 6% DV; Sugar 20g

Orange Apricot Muesli

VEGETARIAN, GLUTEN-FREE

SERVES 4 / **PREP TIME:** 15 minutes

Native to Germany and Switzerland, muesli is a mixture of cereals traditionally served for breakfast. Its base of rolled oats can help lower blood cholesterol. Oat bran, dried fruit, and walnuts add more flavor—and even more fiber.

2 cups regular rolled oats, toasted if desired (see Ingredient Tip)
⅓ cup oat bran
⅓ cup dried chopped apricots
¼ cup chopped walnuts
Pinch salt
1 teaspoon ground cinnamon
¼ cup orange juice
1⅓ cups low-fat almond, soy, or dairy milk

1. In a medium bowl, combine the oats, oat bran, apricots, walnuts, salt, and cinnamon and mix well. Add the orange juice and milk and mix.

2. You can either let this stand for 10 minutes, then serve, or cover the bowl and refrigerate overnight, and stir gently before serving.

INGREDIENT TIP: To toast the oats, spread them in a thin layer on a baking sheet. Bake them in a 350°F oven for about 10 to 15 minutes, stirring once, until they turn a darker color and release a nutty aroma. Cool the oats completely before storing them in an airtight container at room temperature for up to one week.

Per serving: Calories 280; Fat 9g (with 29% calories from fat); Saturated fat 1g; Monounsaturated fat 2g; Carbs 47g; Sodium 66mg; Dietary fiber 7g; Protein 9g; Cholesterol 0mg; Vitamin A 29% DV; Vitamin C 15% DV; Sugar 4g

Cranberry Orange Mixed Grain Granola

VEGAN

MAKES 3 cups (serves 6) / **PREP TIME:** 5 minutes / **COOK TIME:** 20 minutes

Granola makes a great on-the-go breakfast, and this version is healthier than just about anything you can buy at the store. Oats, barley, kamut, and sunflower seeds pack this sweet homemade cereal with heart-healthy fiber.

1 cup regular rolled oats
½ cup barley flakes
1 cup kamut flakes or corn or wheat flakes
⅓ cup sunflower seeds
3 tablespoons pure maple syrup
1 tablespoon safflower oil
1 tablespoon orange juice
1 teaspoon vanilla extract
2 teaspoons fresh orange zest
½ cup chopped dried cranberries

1. Preheat the oven to 350°F.

2. In a large bowl, combine the rolled oats, barley flakes, kamut flakes, and sunflower seeds.

3. In a small bowl, combine the maple syrup, safflower oil, orange juice, vanilla, and orange zest, mixing well.

4. Drizzle the maple syrup mixture over the grains and toss to coat.

5. Spread the mixture in a baking sheet.

6. Bake for 15 to 20 minutes, stirring once, until the mixture is lightly toasted.

7. Stir in the cranberries, let the granola cool completely, and store in an airtight container at room temperature for up to 1 week.

Per serving: Calories 226; Fat 8g (with 32% calories from fat); Saturated fat 1g; Monounsaturated fat 3g; Carbs 39g; Sodium 47mg; Dietary fiber 6g; Protein 5g; Cholesterol 0mg; Vitamin A 3% DV; Vitamin C 2% DV; Sugar 14g

Blueberry Almond Breakfast Bowl

VEGETARIAN, GLUTEN-FREE

SERVES 1 / **PREP TIME:** 15 minutes

Naturally high in fiber, chia seeds pair perfectly with fresh fruit. If you decide to prep this dish in advance (and keep in the refrigerator overnight), you'll find that the chia seeds expand and the breakfast bowl takes on a decadent pudding-like texture.

¾ cup full-fat plain Greek yogurt
⅔ cup blueberries, divided
½ small banana, cut into slices
1 tablespoon chia seeds
2 tablespoons low-fat almond milk
1 tablespoon sliced almonds, toasted

1. In a blender or food processor, combine the yogurt, ¼ cup of the blueberries, the banana, chia seeds, and almond milk. Blend or process until smooth.

2. Spoon into a cereal bowl and top with the almonds and remaining blueberries.

SUBSTITUTION TIP: If you are allergic to almonds, you can substitute soy or dairy milk for the almond milk in this recipe. Instead of the sliced almonds, use chopped toasted walnuts, a nut-free granola blend, or choose other fruit, such as raspberries or blackberries.

Per serving: Calories 343; Fat 15g (with 39% calories from fat); Saturated fat 5g; Monounsaturated fat 1g; Carbs 44g; Sodium 109mg; Dietary fiber 14g; Protein 12g; Cholesterol 24mg; Vitamin A 6% DV; Vitamin C 21% DV; Sugar 23g

Amaranth and Date Porridge

VEGAN, GLUTEN-FREE

SERVES 4 / **PREP TIME:** 5 minutes / **COOK TIME:** 22 minutes

Traditionally a staple in porridge, amaranth is a powerhouse ancient grain from Peru that looks like tiny beads (it's actually a seed, not a grain). This makes for a satisfying breakfast that's also very high in protein and phytosterols, which can help lower total cholesterol and LDL levels.

1 cup amaranth
2½ cups water
½ cup unsweetened apple juice
1 tablespoon pure maple syrup
1 teaspoon canola oil
⅛ teaspoon ground nutmeg
Pinch salt
⅓ cup Medjool dates, pitted and chopped

1. In a medium saucepan, combine the amaranth, water, apple juice, maple syrup, canola oil, nutmeg, and salt.

2. Bring to a boil over medium heat, reduce heat to low, and simmer for 15 minutes, stirring occasionally.

3. Stir the mixture and add the dates.

4. Continue cooking for another 5 to 7 minutes, stirring frequently, or until the porridge is thickened and the amaranth is tender. Serve immediately.

INGREDIENT TIP: While soy milk has double the fat of 1% cow's milk, at 4 grams per cup as opposed to 2 grams, cow's milk has 12 grams of sugar, while soy milk has just 1 gram per cup. Both of these foods are good sources of protein and calcium.

Per serving: 252 calories, Fat 5g (18% calories from fat); Saturated fat 1g; monounsaturated fat 2g; Carbs 47g; Sodium 47mg; Detary fiber 4g, Protein 7g, Cholesterol 0g; Vitamin A 0% DV; Vitamin C 21% DV, Sugar 17g

Curried Farro Hot Cereal

VEGAN, NUT-FREE

SERVES 4 / **PREP TIME:** 5 minutes / **COOK TIME:** 25 minutes

This cereal satisfies if you have a savory and slightly sweet tooth. Farro is an ancient grain that is surging in popularity. Really a type of wheat, farro contains ample fiber, protein, and iron. Curry powder includes turmeric, which has antioxidant compounds for heart health.

1 cup farro
½ cup unsweetened apple juice
1½ cups water
½ cup low-fat soy milk
1 tablespoon pure maple syrup, plus more for serving (optional)
1 to 2 teaspoons curry powder
Pinch salt
⅓ cup dried currants

1. In a medium heavy saucepan, combine the farro, apple juice, water, soy milk, maple syrup, curry powder, and salt. Bring to a simmer over medium heat, then reduce the heat to low.

2. Cover the pot and cook the farro mixture, stirring occasionally, for about 20 minutes. Stir in the currants and cook 5 to 7 minutes longer or until the grains are tender but still chewy.

3. Serve with fresh fruit and a drizzle of maple syrup, if desired.

Per serving: Calories 182; Fat 2g (with 10% calories from fat); Saturated fat 0g; Monounsaturated fat 0g; Carbs 38g; Sodium 15mg; Dietary fiber 3g; Protein 5g; Cholesterol 0mg; Vitamin A 2% DV; Vitamin C 21% DV; Sugar 16g

Spicy Omelet

VEGETARIAN, GLUTEN-FREE, NUT-FREE

SERVES 2 / **PREP TIME:** 15 minutes / **COOK TIME:** 8 minutes

Egg whites make a fluffy and delicious omelet with very little fat, but to some, egg white omelets are not very appealing. You can add just one whole egg (with the yolk) to the omelet and it will lend the appearance of being a true omelet, but will be far healthier! See the Variation Tip for other ideas.

1 whole egg
6 egg whites
1 tablespoon water
¼ teaspoon chili powder
Pinch salt
⅛ teaspoon white pepper
Olive oil cooking spray
½ cup salsa
1 cup arugula or baby spinach leaves

1. In a medium bowl, combine the egg, egg whites, water, chili powder, salt, and white pepper, and beat well with a fork.

2. Spray an 8-inch omelet pan or nonstick skillet with olive oil cooking spray, and heat over medium heat.

3. When a drop of water in the pan skitters, add the egg mixture. Cook over medium heat, shaking the pan occasionally, lifting the edges of the omelet with a nonstick spatula so uncooked egg can flow underneath, and running the spatula around the edge of the pan to make sure the omelet isn't sticking.

4. When the eggs are set but still moist on top, spread the salsa and the arugula or baby spinach evenly across one half. Fold the omelet

in half and slide onto a warmed plate. Cut in half and serve immediately.

Per serving: Calories 109; Fat 3g (with 25% calories from fat); Saturated fat 1g; Monounsaturated fat 1g; Carbs 6g; Sodium 594mg; Dietary fiber 1g; Protein 15g; Cholesterol 106mg; Vitamin A 13% DV; Vitamin C 5% DV; Sugar 3g

Scrambled Egg Tacos

VEGETARIAN, GLUTEN-FREE, NUT-FREE

SERVES 4 / **PREP TIME:** 10 minutes / **COOK TIME:** 10 minutes

This savory breakfast dish also satisfies as a quick dinner. Using mostly egg whites cuts the fat content way down. Meanwhile, the salsa, corn, and lettuce add vitamins and texture, the cheese lends a salty note, and the spices give it a hot kick.

1 whole egg
6 egg whites
1 tablespoon water
1 to 2 teaspoons chili powder
Pinch salt
⅛ teaspoon black pepper
⅛ teaspoon red pepper flakes
1 teaspoon olive oil
4 warmed crisp corn taco shells, or 4 warmed corn or flour tortillas
⅔ cup salsa
¾ cup frozen corn, thawed
2 tablespoons grated cotija cheese
1 cup shredded romaine lettuce

1. In a medium bowl, combine the egg, egg whites, water, chili powder, salt, pepper, and red pepper flakes, and beat thoroughly with a fork until foamy.

2. Heat the olive oil in a medium skillet over medium heat. Add the egg mixture and cook, stirring frequently, until the eggs are cooked through but still moist, about 5 to 7 minutes. Remove from the heat.

3. Meanwhile, warm the taco shells as directed on the package.

4. Divide the egg mixture among the taco shells and top with the salsa, corn, cheese, and lettuce. Serve immediately.

INGREDIENT TIP: Cotija cheese is a sharp Mexican grating cheese that has a strong flavor. A little bit goes a long way. Most supermarkets carry this cheese, or you could visit a Mexican market. It keeps for weeks in the refrigerator. If you can't find it, use shredded or grated Romano or Parmesan cheese.

Per serving: Calories 166; Fat 4g (with 22% calories from fat); Saturated fat 1g; Monounsaturated fat 2g; Carbs 24g; Sodium 413mg; Dietary fiber 4g; Protein 11g; Cholesterol 56mg; Vitamin A 33% DV; Vitamin C 11% DV; Sugar 3g

Asparagus Kale Frittata

VEGETARIAN, GLUTEN-FREE, NUT-FREE

SERVES 3 / **PREP TIME:** 10 minutes / **COOK TIME:** 15 minutes

Simply a sturdy omelet, a frittata can be cooked on the stovetop or baked. Kale and asparagus add fiber and color to this easy and nutritious recipe that comes together in mere minutes.

1 small bunch curly kale
1 teaspoon olive oil
8 asparagus spears, cut into 2-inch pieces
2 tablespoons water
1 whole egg
5 egg whites
1 tablespoon low-fat Greek yogurt
½ teaspoon dried thyme leaves
Pinch salt
⅛ teaspoon white pepper
Pinch turmeric
2 tablespoons crumbled goat cheese

1. Rinse the kale thoroughly and remove the tough center stem. Tear into bite-sized pieces.

2. Heat a 9-inch skillet over medium heat and add the olive oil.

3. When the oil is hot, add the kale and asparagus and sauté, stirring frequently, for 3 minutes.

4. Add the water, cover the pan, and let steam for 2 minutes.

5. Meanwhile, in a medium bowl, beat the egg, egg whites, yogurt, thyme, salt, pepper, and turmeric. Stir in the cheese.

6. Uncover the pan and add the egg mixture to the vegetables. Cook over medium heat, shaking the pan, lifting the edges with a spatula so uncooked egg can flow underneath, and running a spatula around the edges, until the eggs are set. Serve immediately.

SUBSTITUTION TIP: When asparagus isn't in season, you can substitute other veggies in this easy recipe. Try chopped or sliced zucchini, yellow summer squash, broccoli florets, or chopped bell peppers. If you don't like kale, you can substitute baby spinach leaves, collard greens, Swiss chard, or broccoli rabe.

Per serving: Calories 120; Fat 5g (with 38% calories from fat); Saturated fat 2g; Monounsaturated fat 2g; Carbs 9g; Sodium 176mg; Dietary fiber 2g; Protein 12g; Cholesterol 73mg; Vitamin A 215% DV; Vitamin C 138% DV; Sugar 2g

Nutty Quinoa Waffles

VEGETARIAN, GLUTEN-FREE

SERVES 4 / **PREP TIME:** 10 minutes / **COOK TIME:** 15 minutes

Quinoa is packed with protein and fiber, and in flour form, it's very versatile. It will keep you feeling full and help reduce cholesterol. It adds an irresistible nutty flavor to these crisp and tender waffles. You can find quinoa flour at large supermarkets and online.

1 cup quinoa flour
1½ teaspoons baking powder
1 teaspoon ground cinnamon
⅛ teaspoon ground nutmeg
Pinch salt
1 egg, separated
½ cup almond or soy milk
2 tablespoons honey or pure maple syrup
1 teaspoon vanilla extract
3 tablespoons ground pecans

1. In a medium bowl, combine the quinoa flour, baking powder, cinnamon, nutmeg, and salt and blend well with a wire whisk or fork.

2. In a small bowl, combine the egg yolk, almond milk, honey, and vanilla and mix well.

3. In another medium bowl, beat the egg white until stiff.

4. Stir the egg yolk mixture into the dry ingredients, then fold in the egg white.

5. Preheat a waffle iron and spray it with nonstick cooking spray.

6. Add batter to the waffle iron per the manufacturer's instructions. Close the iron and cook until the steaming stops, 4 to 5 minutes.

Remove the waffle from the iron, sprinkle with ground pecans, and serve immediately.

Per serving: Calories 195; Fat 7g (with 32% calories from fat); Saturated fat 1g; Monounsaturated fat 3g; Carbs 30g; Sodium 169mg; Dietary fiber 4g; Protein 6g; Cholesterol 53mg; Vitamin A 2% DV; Vitamin C 0% DV; Sugar 10g

Cinnamon Oat Bran Banana Pancakes

VEGETARIAN, GLUTEN-FREE, NUT-FREE

SERVES 4 / **PREP TIME:** 15 minutes / **COOK TIME:** 15 minutes

This recipe improves on the flavor of a classic pancake with the addition of cinnamon and bananas. By including oat bran (the outer hull of the oat groat, which is very high in fiber), you also fight cholesterol.

1 cup gluten-free flour blend (regular/ whole-wheat flour if you prefer)
⅓ cup oat bran
1 tablespoon brown sugar
1 teaspoon ground cinnamon
½ teaspoon baking powder
½ teaspoon baking soda
1 small banana, peeled and mashed
⅔ cup low-fat milk
1 egg, separated
1 tablespoon canola oil

1. In a medium bowl, combine the flour, oat bran, brown sugar, cinnamon, baking powder, and baking soda and mix well with a wire whisk.

2. In another medium bowl, combine the banana, milk, and egg yolk, and beat until well combined.

3. In another medium bowl, beat the egg white with an electric mixer until stiff peaks form.

4. Add the banana mixture to the flour mixture and stir just until combined. Do not overmix.

5. Fold in the beaten egg white.

6. Heat a nonstick griddle or large skillet over medium heat, add the oil, and swirl it around the pan. When the pan is hot enough that a drop of water skitters on the surface, pour a scant ¼ cup of the batter onto the griddle. Repeat to just fill the pan.

7. Cook the pancakes until the edges start to look lightly browned and bubbles form on the surface, about 2 minutes. Flip the pancakes and cook for 1 to 2 minutes longer or until the bottoms are browned. Serve immediately.

INGREDIENT TIP: If you cannot eat gluten, purchase certified gluten-free oats and oat bran. That means the oats were grown far away from wheat fields and are processed in a dedicated mill to avoid cross-contamination. The most responsible processors will have the oats tested for any gluten residue. The oats should be marked "gluten-free" on the package.

Per serving: Calories 245; Fat 6g (with 22% calories from fat); Saturated fat 1g; Monounsaturated fat 3g; Carbs 44g; Sodium 241mg; Dietary fiber 2g; Protein 7g; Cholesterol 55mg; Vitamin A 3% DV; Vitamin C 5% DV; Sugar 6g

Baked French Toast Strips with Mixed Berry Sauce

VEGETARIAN, NUT-FREE

SERVES 4 / **PREP TIME:** 10 minutes / **COOK TIME:** 20 minutes

This breakfast favorite gets a healthy and fun twist in this easy recipe. The bread is cut into strips for dipping into a vitamin- and fiber-filled sweet-tart berry sauce. You get to choose between gluten-free or whole-wheat slices.

4 slices whole-wheat or gluten-free bread
½ cup low-fat soy or dairy milk
2 teaspoons brown sugar
1 egg
1 egg white
1 teaspoon vanilla extract
½ cup raspberries
½ cup sliced strawberries
1 tablespoon orange juice

1. Preheat the oven to 375°F. Line a baking sheet with parchment paper.

2. Cut the bread into four strips each; set aside.

3. In a shallow bowl, combine the milk, brown sugar, egg, egg white, and vanilla, and beat until frothy.

4. Dip the bread strips into the milk mixture, turning once. Let the strips sit in the egg mixture for 1 minute. Remove and place on the prepared baking sheet.

5. Bake the strips for 15 to 20 minutes, until crisp and golden brown.

6. Meanwhile, combine the raspberries, strawberries, and orange juice in a small bowl. Mash until combined. (You can also prepare this sauce in a blender.)

7. When the French toast strips are done, serve immediately with the sauce on the side.

Per serving: Calories 131; Fat 3g (with 21% calories from fat); Saturated fat 1g; Monounsaturated fat 1g; Carbs 19g; Sodium 182mg; Dietary fiber 3g; Protein 8g; Cholesterol 54mg; Vitamin A 3% DV; Vitamin C 31% DV; Sugar 5g

Shrimp and Pineapple Lettuce Wraps

CHAPTER THREE

Fish and Seafood

Roasted Shrimp and Veggies

Shrimp and Pineapple Lettuce Wraps

Grilled Scallops with Gremolata

Healthy Paella

Vietnamese Fish and Noodle Bowl

Cod Satay

Crispy Mixed Nut Fish Fillets

Steamed Sole Rolls with Greens

Red Snapper Scampi

Orange Thyme Red Snapper

Mediterranean Roasted Mahi Mahi with Broccoli

Catalán Salmon Tacos

Salmon with Farro Pilaf

Salmon with Spicy Mixed Beans

Arctic Char with Tomato Pear Compote

Roasted Shrimp and Veggies

PESCATARIAN, GLUTEN-FREE, NUT-FREE

SERVES 4 / **PREP TIME:** 10 minutes / **COOK TIME:** 20 minutes

A one-pan dinner lets you quickly get a weekday meal on the table without a lot of effort. And by purchasing precut veggies, you can speed it up even more. Featuring a nutrient-dense variety of ingredients—mushrooms, potatoes, broccoli, garlic, green beans, and cauliflower—this recipe satisfies.

1 cup sliced cremini mushrooms
2 medium chopped Yukon Gold potatoes, rinsed, unpeeled
2 cups broccoli florets
3 cloves garlic, sliced
1 cup sliced fresh green beans
1 cup cauliflower florets
2 tablespoons fresh lemon juice
2 tablespoons low-sodium vegetable broth
1 teaspoon olive oil
1 teaspoon dried thyme
½ teaspoon dried oregano
Pinch salt
⅛ teaspoon black pepper
½ pound medium shrimp, peeled and deveined

1. Preheat the oven to 400°F.

2. In a large baking pan, combine the mushrooms, potatoes, broccoli, garlic, green beans, and cauliflower, and toss to coat.

3. In a small bowl, combine the lemon juice, broth, olive oil, thyme, oregano, salt, and pepper and mix well. Drizzle over the vegetables

4. Roast for 15 minutes, then stir.

5. Add the shrimp and distribute evenly.

6. Roast for another 5 minutes or until the shrimp curl and turn pink. Serve immediately.

INGREDIENT TIP: You can save lots of time in the kitchen by buying prepared broccoli, cauliflower florets, and sliced mushrooms to use in recipes like this one. Make sure the vegetables aren't seasoned and that they look fresh.

Per serving: Calories 192; Fat 3g (with 14% calories from fat); Saturated fat 0g; Monounsaturated fat 1g; Carbs 29g; Sodium 116mg; Dietary fiber 5g; Protein 17g; Cholesterol 86mg; Vitamin A 12% DV; Vitamin C 138% DV; Sugar 3g

Shrimp and Pineapple Lettuce Wraps

PESCATARIAN, GLUTEN-FREE, NUT-FREE

SERVES 4 / **PREP TIME:** 15 minutes / **COOK TIME:** 12 minutes

These low-fat, high-protein wraps make for a perfect portable lunch; romaine or Boston lettuce leaves encase the sweet and spicy filling. Pineapple adds a hearty dose of fiber and vitamin C.

2 teaspoons olive oil
2 jalapeño peppers, seeded and minced
6 scallions, chopped
2 yellow bell peppers, seeded and chopped
8 ounces small shrimp, peeled and deveined
2 cups canned pineapple chunks, drained, reserving juice
2 tablespoons fresh lime juice
1 avocado, peeled, and cubed
1 large carrot, coarsely grated
8 romaine or Boston lettuce leaves, rinsed and dried

1. In a medium saucepan, heat the olive oil over medium heat.

2. Add the jalapeño pepper and scallions and cook for 2 minutes, stirring constantly.

3. Add the bell pepper, and cook for 2 minutes.

4. Add the shrimp, and cook for 1 minute, stirring constantly.

5. Add the pineapple, 2 tablespoons of the reserved pineapple juice, and lime juice, and bring to a simmer. Simmer for 1 minute longer or until the shrimp curl and turn pink. Let the mixture cool for 5 minutes.

6. Serve the shrimp mixture with the cubed avocado and grated carrot, wrapped in the lettuce leaves.

COOKING TIP: You can make the shrimp mixture up to 2 hours ahead of time; any longer, and the shrimp may become mushy. Store the mixture covered in the fridge. Warm the filling if you'd like or serve it cold or at room temperature.

Per serving: Calories 241; Fat 9g (with 33% calories from fat); Saturated fat 2g; Monounsaturated fat 5g; Carbs 29g; Sodium 109mg; Dietary fiber 6g; Protein 6g; Cholesterol 109mg; Vitamin A 96% DV; Vitamin C 332% DV; Sugar 16g

Grilled Scallops with Gremolata

PESCATARIAN, GLUTEN-FREE, NUT-FREE

SERVES 4 / **PREP TIME:** 15 minutes / **COOK TIME:** 6 minutes

This entrée is perfect for summer nights when you want to eat outside. A naturally low-fat shellfish, scallops come in two varieties: bay and sea—bay scallops are smaller, since a bay is smaller than the sea.

2 scallions, cut into pieces
¾ cup packed fresh flat-leaf parsley
¼ cup packed fresh basil leaves
1 teaspoon lemon zest
3 tablespoons fresh lemon juice
1 tablespoon olive oil
20 sea scallops
2 teaspoons butter, melted
Pinch salt
⅛ teaspoon lemon pepper

1. Prepare and preheat the grill to medium-high. Make sure the grill rack is clean.

2. Meanwhile, make the gremolata. In a blender or food processor, combine the scallions, parsley, basil, lemon zest, lemon juice, and olive oil. Blend or process until the herbs are finely chopped. Pour into a small bowl and set aside.

3. Put the scallops on a plate. If the scallops have a small tough muscle attached to them, remove and discard it. Brush the melted butter over the scallops. Sprinkle with the salt and the lemon pepper.

4. Place the scallops in a grill basket, if you have one. If not, place a sheet of heavy-duty foil on the grill, punch some holes in it, and

arrange the scallops evenly across it.

5. Grill the scallops for 2 to 3 minutes per side, turning once, until opaque. Drizzle with the gremolata and serve.

SUBSTITUTION TIP: Classic gremolata is a garnish made with just parsley, lemon, garlic, and lots of oil. The oil is greatly reduced in this recipe, but it's just as tasty as the original. You could omit the scallions or add any type of green herb you'd like to this recipe. Try using fresh thyme leaves, fresh oregano leaves, mint, or even sage.

Per serving: Calories 190; Fat 7g (with 33% calories from fat); Saturated fat 2g; Monounsaturated fat 3g; Carbs 2g; Sodium 336mg; Dietary fiber 1g; Protein 28g; Cholesterol 68mg; Vitamin A 27% DV; Vitamin C 37% DV; Sugar 1g

Healthy Paella

PESCATARIAN, GLUTEN-FREE, NUT-FREE

SERVES 4 / **PREP TIME:** 15 minutes / **COOK TIME:** 15 minutes

Paella is a Spanish one-dish meal typically made with rice, chicken, chorizo, and several different kinds of fish and shellfish. It also takes close to an hour to perfect. This simplified and lightened-up version cooks up in half the time and features vegetables and whole-wheat pasta for added fiber.

1 tablespoon olive oil
1 onion, chopped
3 cloves garlic, minced
1 red bell pepper, seeded and chopped
2½ cups low-sodium vegetable broth
1 tomato, chopped
1 teaspoon smoked paprika
1 teaspoon dried thyme leaves
¼ teaspoon turmeric
⅛ teaspoon black pepper
1 cup whole-wheat orzo
½ pound halibut fillets, cut into 1-inch pieces
12 medium shrimp, peeled and deveined
¼ cup chopped fresh flat-leaf parsley

1. In a large deep skillet, heat the olive oil over medium heat.

2. Add the onion, garlic, and red bell pepper, and cook, stirring, for 2 minutes.

3. Add the vegetable broth, tomato, paprika, thyme, turmeric, and black pepper, and bring to a simmer.

4. Stir in the orzo, making sure it is submerged in the liquid in the pan. Simmer for 5 minutes, stirring occasionally.

5. Add the halibut and stir. Simmer for 4 minutes.

6. Add the shrimp and stir. Simmer for 2 to 3 minutes or until the shrimp curl and turn pink and the pasta is cooked al dente.

7. Sprinkle with the parsley, and serve immediately.

SUBSTITUTION TIP: Paella is typically served with cooked arborio rice, but we use whole-wheat orzo in this recipe to add more fiber and nutrition and to cut down on the cooking time. If you would like to use brown rice, omit the orzo, cook the rice separately, and serve the paella over the rice.

Per serving: Calories 367; Fat 7g (with 17% calories from fat); Saturated fat 1g; Monounsaturated fat 3g; Carbs 50g; Sodium 147mg; Dietary fiber 9g; Protein 25g; Cholesterol 50mg; Vitamin A 38% DV; Vitamin C 84% DV; Sugar 5g

Vietnamese Fish and Noodle Bowl

PESCATARIAN

SERVES 3 / **PREP TIME:** 15 minutes / **COOK TIME:** 15 minutes

Ingredients commonly used in Vietnamese cooking include garlic, fish sauce, red pepper flakes, daikon radish, cilantro, basil, and mint. These flavors come together beautifully in this simple, heart-healthy noodle bowl.

¾ pound grouper fillets, cut into 1-inch pieces
1 tablespoon cornstarch
⅛ teaspoon cayenne pepper
2 teaspoons fish sauce
1 tablespoon rice wine vinegar
1 teaspoon sugar
2 tablespoons fresh lemon juice
1 teaspoon olive oil
¼ cup minced daikon radish
3 cloves garlic, minced
4 ounces whole-wheat spaghetti, broken in half
1½ cups low-sodium vegetable broth
2 tablespoons chopped peanuts
2 tablespoons minced fresh cilantro
2 tablespoons minced fresh basil

1. In a medium bowl, toss the grouper with the cornstarch and cayenne pepper and set aside.

2. In a small bowl, combine the fish sauce, rice wine vinegar, sugar, and lemon juice, and stir to mix well.

3. In a large skillet, heat the olive oil over medium heat. Add the daikon and garlic and cook for 1 minute, stirring constantly.

4. Add the fish to the skillet; sauté for 2 to 3 minutes, stirring frequently, until the fish browns lightly.

5. Remove the fish mixture to a large bowl and set aside.

6. Add the spaghetti and vegetable broth to the skillet, and stir. Bring to a simmer over high heat and cook for 7 to 8 minutes or until the pasta is al dente.

7. Return the fish and radish mixture to the skillet along with the fish sauce mixture, peanuts, cilantro, and basil. Toss for 1 minute, then serve immediately in bowls.

SUBSTITUTION TIP: If you prefer, you can substitute the fish sauce with some low-sodium soy sauce, hoisin, or miso and minced garlic. You can also omit the peanuts for a nut-free recipe.

Per serving: Calories 324; Fat 6g (with 17% calories from fat); Saturated fat 1g; Monounsaturated fat 3g; Carbs 38g; Sodium 439mg; Dietary fiber 1g; Protein 30g; Cholesterol 46mg; Vitamin A 7% DV; Vitamin C 12% DV; Sugar 3g

Cod Satay

PESCATARIAN

SERVES 4 / **PREP TIME:** 15 minutes / **COOK TIME:** 15 minutes

Cod is a widely available white fish that's low-fat and heart-healthy. Here, it's served with an aromatic Indian-style satay sauce made with tomato, spices, coconut milk, and peanut butter.

2 teaspoons olive oil, divided
1 small onion, diced
2 cloves garlic, minced
⅓ cup low-fat coconut milk
1 tomato, chopped
2 tablespoons low-fat peanut butter
1 tablespoon packed brown sugar
⅓ cup low-sodium vegetable broth
2 teaspoons low-sodium soy sauce
⅛ teaspoon ground ginger
Pinch red pepper flakes
4 (6-ounce) cod fillets
⅛ teaspoon white pepper

1. In a small saucepan, heat 1 teaspoon of the olive oil over medium heat.

2. Add the onion and garlic, and cook, stirring frequently for 3 minutes.

3. Add the coconut milk, tomato, peanut butter, brown sugar, broth, soy sauce, ginger, and red pepper flakes, and bring to a simmer, stirring with a whisk until the sauce combines. Simmer for 2 minutes, then remove the satay sauce from the heat and set aside.

4. Season the cod with the white pepper.

5. Heat a large nonstick skillet with the remaining 1 teaspoon olive oil, and add the cod fillets. Cook for 3 minutes, then turn and cook for 3 to 4 minutes more or until the fish flakes when tested with a fork.

6. Cover the fish with the satay sauce and serve immediately.

INGREDIENT TIP: Watch out for sodium levels in frozen cod fillets. Many have added sodium tripolyphosphate, which is used to retain moisture, but this can significantly increase the sodium content. The best cod is fresh wild-caught fillets.

Per serving: Calories 255; Fat 10g (with 35% calories from fat); Saturated fat 5g; Monounsaturated fat 3g; Carbs 9g; Sodium 222mg; Dietary fiber 1g; Protein 33g; Cholesterol 72mg; Vitamin A 4% DV; Vitamin C 9% DV; Sugar 4g

Crispy Mixed Nut Fish Fillets

PESCATARIAN, GLUTEN-FREE

SERVES 4 / **PREP TIME:** 10 minutes / **COOK TIME:** 15 minutes

Plain white fish fillets can be made more exciting with the addition of seasonings and coatings. In this recipe, tender fish is encased in a crisp high-fiber nut coating that has a mustardy zing.

4 (6-ounce) white fish fillets, such as red snapper or cod
2 tablespoons low-sodium yellow mustard
2 tablespoons nonfat plain Greek yogurt
2 tablespoons low-fat buttermilk
1 teaspoon dried Italian herb seasoning
⅛ teaspoon white pepper
¼ cup hazelnut flour
2 tablespoons almond flour
2 tablespoons ground almonds
2 tablespoons ground hazelnuts

1. Preheat the oven to 400°F. Line a baking sheet with a fine wire rack and set aside.

2. Pat the fish dry and place on a plate.

3. In a shallow bowl, combine the mustard, yogurt, buttermilk, Italian seasoning, and white pepper.

4. On a plate, combine the hazelnut flour and almond flour, and add the ground almonds, the ground hazelnuts, and mix well.

5. Coat the fish with the mustard mixture, then coat with the nut mixture. Place on the prepared baking sheet.

6. Bake the fish for 12 to 17 minutes, until it flakes when tested with a fork. Serve immediately.

COOKING TIP: Lining the baking sheet with a wire rack allows the oven heat to circulate around the fish as it cooks. Not only does this mean the fish cooks more evenly, but the nut coating on the bottom of the fish will be as crisp as the coating on the top.

Per serving: Calories 256; Fat 9g (with 32% calories from fat); Saturated fat 1g; Monounsaturated fat 5g; Carbs 4g; Sodium 206mg; Dietary fiber 2g; Protein 38g; Cholesterol 63mg; Vitamin A 4% DV; Vitamin C 6% DV; Sugar 2g

Steamed Sole Rolls with Greens

PESCATARIAN

SERVES 4 / **PREP TIME:** 15 minutes / **COOK TIME:** 10 minutes

Sole is a very delicate and mild white fish. It's delicious in this elegant dish, featuring the Asian-inspired flavors of ginger, garlic, soy, and toasted sesame. The vegetables supply added nutrition, color, and soluble fiber.

4 (6-ounce) sole fillets
2 teaspoons grated peeled fresh ginger root
2 cloves garlic, minced
2 teaspoons low-sodium soy sauce
1 tablespoon rice wine vinegar
1 teaspoon toasted sesame oil
2 cups fresh torn spinach leaves
1 cup fresh stemmed torn kale
1 cup sliced mushrooms
2 teaspoons toasted sesame seeds

1. Cut the sole fillets in half lengthwise. Sprinkle each piece with some of the ginger root and garlic. Roll up the fillets, ginger root side in. Fasten with a toothpick and set aside.

2. In a small bowl, combine the soy sauce, vinegar, and toasted sesame oil.

3. Bring water to a boil over medium heat in a large shallow saucepan that will hold your steamer.

4. Arrange the spinach leaves and kale in the bottom of the steamer. Add the rolled sole fillets. Add the mushrooms, and sprinkle everything with the soy sauce mixture.

5. Cover and steam for 7 to 11 minutes or until the fish is cooked and flakes when tested with a fork. Remove the toothpicks.

6. To serve, sprinkle with the sesame seeds and serve the fish on top of the wilted greens and mushrooms.

COOKING TIP: If you don't have a collapsible steamer, you can use a metal colander placed over a pot of simmering water. Make sure the bottom of the colander that holds the food doesn't touch the water as it simmers and you've covered it with a lid.

Per serving: Calories 263; Fat 8g (with 27% calories from fat); Saturated fat 2g; Monounsaturated fat 3g; Carbs 7g; Sodium 247mg; Dietary fiber 3g; Protein 36g; Cholesterol 81mg; Vitamin A 81% DV; Vitamin C 47% DV; Sugar 0g

Red Snapper Scampi

PESCATARIAN, GLUTEN-FREE, NUT-FREE

SERVES 4 / **PREP TIME:** 10 minutes / **COOK TIME:** 20 minutes

Scampi is traditionally served with a heaping plate of pasta or a hunk of crusty bread, but this slimmed-down recipe omits pasta and bread, and lets the lemon-garlic sauce take the spotlight. The result? A low-fat, high-protein entrée.

2 teaspoons olive oil
4 cloves garlic, minced
¼ cup fresh lemon juice
¼ cup white wine or fish stock
1 teaspoon fresh lemon zest
Pinch salt
⅛ teaspoon lemon pepper
4 (6-ounce) red snapper fillets
2 scallions, minced
3 tablespoons minced flat-leaf fresh parsley

1. Preheat the oven to 400°F. Line a baking pan with parchment paper.

2. In a small bowl, combine the olive oil, garlic, lemon juice, white wine, lemon zest, salt, and lemon pepper.

3. Arrange the fillets skin side down, if the skin is attached, on the prepared baking pan. Pour the lemon juice mixture over the fillets.

4. Roast for 15 to 20 minutes, or until the fish flakes when tested with a fork.

5. Serve the fish with the pan drippings, sprinkled with the scallions and parsley.

Per serving: Calories 212; Fat 5g (with 21% calories from fat); Saturated fat 1g; Monounsaturated fat 2g; Carbs 3g; Sodium 112mg; Dietary fiber 0g; Protein 35g; Cholesterol 62mg; Vitamin A 10% DV; Vitamin C 26% DV; Sugar 1g

Orange Thyme Red Snapper

PESCATARIAN, GLUTEN-FREE, NUT-FREE

SERVES 4 / **PREP TIME:** 5 minutes / **COOK TIME:** 10 minutes

Red snapper is a mild white fish that's a great source of vitamin B_{12}, which can help lower cholesterol. When paired with sweet and tart orange juice and fragrant fresh thyme, you are in for an elegant meal.

1 medium orange
2 teaspoons olive oil
4 (6-ounce) fillets red snapper
Pinch salt
⅛ teaspoon white pepper
2 teaspoons olive oil
2 scallions, chopped
1½ teaspoons fresh thyme leaves, or ½ teaspoon dried

1. Rinse the orange and dry. Using a small grater or zester, remove 1 teaspoon zest from the orange and set aside. Cut the orange in half, squeeze in a small bowl, and reserve the juice.

2. Add the olive oil to a large nonstick skillet and place over medium heat. Meanwhile, sprinkle the fish with the salt and white pepper.

3. Add the fish to the skillet, skin-side down, if the skin is attached. Cook 3 minutes on one side, briefly pressing on the fish with a spatula to prevent curling (or slit the fillet to prevent curling). Turn the fish and cook for 2 to 3 minutes on the second side, until the fish flakes when tested with a fork.

4. Transfer the fish to a plate. Remove the skin, if present, and discard. Cover the fish with a foil tent to keep it warm.

5. Add the scallions and the thyme to the skillet; cook and stir gently for 1 minute. Add the reserved orange juice and orange zest and

simmer for 2 to 3 minutes or until the liquid is slightly reduced.

6. Pour the sauce over the fish and serve immediately.

Per serving: Calories 232; Fat 7g (with 27% calories from fat); Saturated fat 1g; Monounsaturated fat 4g; Carbs 6g; Sodium 121mg; Dietary fiber 1g; Protein 35g; Cholesterol 62mg; Vitamin A 7% DV; Vitamin C 48% DV; Sugar 5g

Mediterranean Roasted Mahi Mahi with Broccoli

PESCATARIAN, GLUTEN-FREE, NUT-FREE

SERVES 4 / **PREP TIME:** 5 minutes / **COOK TIME:** 22 minutes

In this dish, classic Mediterranean flavors complement the mild flavor and moist texture of mahi mahi. The fish is roasted with broccoli and garlic, two heart-healthy foods, in this easy recipe, and a bit of feta cheese is added at the end for a burst of flavor.

2 cups broccoli florets

2 tablespoons olive oil, divided

4 (6-ounce) mahi mahi fillets

1 cup cherry tomatoes

2 cloves peeled garlic, sliced

⅛ teaspoon white pepper

1 teaspoon paprika

2 tablespoons fresh lemon juice

2 tablespoons crumbled feta cheese

1. Preheat the oven to 400°F. Line a baking sheet with parchment paper.

2. Place the broccoli florets on the prepared baking sheet. Drizzle with 1 tablespoon of the olive oil and toss to coat. Spread the broccoli in a single layer.

3. Roast the broccoli for 10 minutes.

4. Remove the baking sheet from the oven. Move the broccoli over to make room for the fish. Place the fish, cherry tomatoes, and garlic on the baking sheet. Sprinkle the fish with the white pepper and paprika.

5. In a small bowl, combine the lemon juice and the remaining 1 tablespoon olive oil, and drizzle over the fish and vegetable

mixture.

6. Roast for 10 to 12 minutes longer, or until the fish flakes when tested with a fork and the broccoli is tender.

7. Sprinkle with the feta cheese and serve immediately.

Per serving: Calories 258; Fat 11g (with 38% calories from fat); Saturated fat 2g; Monounsaturated fat 6g; Carbs 6g; Sodium 171mg; Dietary fiber 2g; Protein 33g; Cholesterol 72mg; Vitamin A 18% DV; Vitamin C 82% DV; Sugar 2g

Catalán Salmon Tacos

PESCATARIAN, GLUTEN-FREE

SERVES 4 / **PREP TIME:** 10 minutes / **COOK TIME:** 20 minutes

Catalán cuisine is similar to Spanish cuisine. You'll find ingredients such as garlic, fresh fish, tomatoes, white beans, onions, raisins, and pine nuts, all of which are heart healthy. This fusion recipe serves up traditional Catalán flavors in a Mexican-inspired package.

1 teaspoon olive oil
1 (6-ounce) salmon fillet
1 teaspoon chili powder
½ teaspoon dried oregano leaves
⅛ teaspoon black pepper
1 small onion, diced
2 cloves peeled garlic, minced
1 (16-ounce) can low-sodium white beans, rinsed and drained
1 tomato, chopped
1 cup torn fresh Swiss chard leaves
2 tablespoons pine nuts
4 corn tortillas, heated

1. Add the olive oil to a large nonstick skillet and place over medium heat. Rub the salmon fillet with the chili powder, oregano, and pepper.

2. Add the salmon to the pan, skin side down. Cook for 3 minutes, then turn and cook for 5 minutes longer, or until the fish flakes when tested with a fork. Remove the salmon from the pan, flake, and set aside.

3. Add the onion and garlic to the pan and cook for 2 to 3 minutes, stirring frequently, until softened.

4. Add the beans and mash some of them into the onions. Cook for 1 minute, stirring occasionally.

5. Add the tomato and Swiss chard and cook for another 1 to 2 minutes until the greens start to wilt. Add the pine nuts to the mixture.

6. Make the tacos by adding the bean mixture and the salmon to the corn tortillas, and fold them in half. Serve immediately.

Per serving: Calories 296; Fat 8g (with 24% calories from fat); Saturated fat 1g; Monounsaturated fat 3g; Carbs 39g; Sodium 63mg; Dietary fiber 8g; Protein 19g; Cholesterol 23mg; Vitamin A 20% DV; Vitamin C 15% DV; Sugar 2g

Salmon with Farro Pilaf

PESCATARIAN, NUT-FREE

SERVES 4 / **PREP TIME:** 5 minutes / **COOK TIME:** 25 minutes

Farro, an ancient grain, makes a healthy—and tasty—pilaf that's full of fiber, protein, and B vitamins as well as iron, magnesium, and zinc. Here, it's combined with dried cherries and currants for an elegant meal that's special enough for company.

½ cup farro
1 ¼ cups low-sodium vegetable broth
4 (4-ounce) salmon fillets
Pinch salt
½ teaspoon dried marjoram leaves
⅛ teaspoon white pepper
¼ cup dried cherries
¼ cup dried currants
1 cup fresh baby spinach leaves
1 tablespoon orange juice

1. Preheat the oven to 400°F. Line a baking sheet with parchment paper and set aside.

2. In a medium saucepan over medium heat, combine the farro and the vegetable broth and bring to a simmer. Reduce the heat to low and simmer, partially covered, for 25 minutes, or until the farro is tender.

3. Meanwhile, sprinkle the salmon with the salt, marjoram, and white pepper and place on the prepared baking sheet.

4. When the farro has cooked for 10 minutes, bake the salmon in the oven for 12 to 15 minutes, or until the salmon flakes when tested with a fork. Remove and cover to keep warm.

5. When the farro is tender, add the cherries, currants, spinach, and orange juice; stir and cover. Let stand off the heat for 2 to 3 minutes.

6. Plate the salmon and serve with the farro pilaf.

INGREDIENT TIP: If you are eating greens such as baby spinach, kale, or arugula raw that haven't been processed and placed in a sealed bag, rinse them well before eating for food safety reasons. But if the greens are cooked or heated, it's not necessary to rinse them unless they are sandy.

Per serving: Calories 304; Fat 8g (with 24% calories from fat); Saturated fat 1g; Monounsaturated fat 2g; Carbs 32g; Sodium 139mg; Dietary fiber 3g; Protein 26g; Cholesterol 62mg; Vitamin A 12% DV; Vitamin C 2% DV; Sugar 17g

Salmon with Spicy Mixed Beans

PESCATARIAN, GLUTEN-FREE, NUT-FREE

SERVES 4 / **PREP TIME:** 5 minutes / **COOK TIME:** 20 minutes

Heart-healthy salmon has become so popular, it's easy to find and makes for a great freezer staple. It adapts beautifully to many seasonings and contains ample omega-3 fatty acids, which can help lower your risk of heart disease.

2 teaspoons olive oil, divided
4 (4-ounce) salmon fillets
Pinch salt
⅛ teaspoon black pepper
1 onion, diced
3 cloves peeled garlic, minced
1 jalapeño pepper, seeded and minced
1 (16-ounce) can low-sodium mixed beans, rinsed and drained
2 tablespoons low-fat plain Greek yogurt
2 tablespoons minced fresh cilantro

1. Put 1 teaspoon of the olive oil in a large skillet and heat over medium heat.

2. Sprinkle the salmon fillets with the salt and pepper and add to the skillet, skin side down.

3. Cook for 5 minutes, then flip the fillets with a spatula and cook for another 3 to 4 minutes or until the salmon flakes when tested with a fork. Remove the fish to a clean warm plate, and cover with an aluminum foil tent to keep warm.

4. Add the remaining 1 teaspoon of the olive oil to the skillet. Add the onion, garlic, and jalapeño pepper; cook, stirring frequently, for 3 minutes.

5. Add the beans and mash with a fork until desired consistency.

6. Remove the pan from the heat, add the yogurt, and stir until combined.

7. Pile the beans onto a serving platter, top with the fish, and sprinkle with the cilantro. Serve immediately.

SUBSTITUTION TIP: If you can't find canned mixed beans, you can substitute a can of cannellini beans, white beans, or even great northern beans. Drain the beans in a colander, then rinse with cool water. Drain again, and they are ready to eat or use in recipes.

Per serving: Calories 293; Fat 10g (with 30% calories from fat); Saturated fat 2g; Monounsaturated fat 4g; Carbs 23g; Sodium 345mg; Dietary fiber 7g; Protein 29g; Cholesterol 62mg; Vitamin A 2% DV; Vitamin C 10% DV; Sugar 4g

Arctic Char with Tomato Pear Compote

PESCATARIAN, GLUTEN-FREE, NUT-FREE

SERVES 4 / **PREP TIME:** 5 minutes / **COOK TIME:** 25 minutes

Arctic char is a relatively unfamiliar fish to most consumers. Rich in omega-3 fatty acids, it is related to salmon and trout and is the northernmost freshwater fish in the world. This preparation pairs it with a simple, savory-sweet compote.

1 scallion, minced
1 pint cherry tomatoes
1 ripe pear, cored and chopped
1 teaspoon olive oil
2 tablespoons fresh lemon juice
1 tablespoon honey
4 (4-ounce) arctic char fillets
Pinch salt
⅛ teaspoon white pepper
2 tablespoons chopped fresh mint

1. Preheat the oven to 400°F. Line a baking sheet with parchment paper.

2. Combine the scallion, cherry tomatoes, and pear on the prepared baking sheet and toss to mix. Drizzle with the olive oil, lemon juice, and honey, and toss again.

3. Roast for 10 minutes, then remove and stir. Make room for the fish fillets on the pan.

4. Place the fish fillets skin side down in the pan. Return the pan to the oven and roast for 12 to 15 minutes or until the cherry tomatoes are soft with brown spots and the fish flakes when tested with a fork.

5. Remove the pan from the oven. Use a spatula to lift the fish fillets off the skin and place on a warmed serving platter.

6. Toss the roasted fruits with the mint and serve with the fish.

DID YOU KNOW? Most arctic char sold in this country is farm-raised. It's also known as alpine trout or sea trout. Because the fish is relatively high in healthy fat, it's a good choice for roasting or broiling since it won't dry out.

Per serving: Calories 228; Fat 8g (with 32% calories from fat); Saturated fat 1g; Monounsaturated fat 3g; Carbs 15g; Sodium 54mg; Dietary fiber 2g; Protein 24g; Cholesterol 62mg; Vitamin A 14% DV; Vitamin C 25% DV; Sugar 11g

Grilled Turkey and Veggie Kabobs

CHAPTER FOUR

Poultry

Crunchy Chicken Coleslaw Salad

Mixed Berry Chicken Salad

Hawaiian Chicken Stir-Fry

Pineapple Curried Chicken

Basil Chicken Meatballs

Mustard-Roasted Almond Chicken Tenders

Nutty Coconut Chicken with Fruit Sauce

"Butter" Chicken

Moroccan Chicken

Piri Piri Chicken

Mini Turkey Meatloaves

Grilled Turkey and Veggie Kabobs

Lemon Tarragon Turkey Medallions

Tandoori Turkey Pizzas

Turkey Tacos Verde

Crunchy Chicken Coleslaw Salad

GLUTEN-FREE

SERVES 4 / **PREP TIME:** 23 minutes / **COOK TIME:** 7 minutes

Chicken salads give you the flexibility of adding flavor and texture to a healthy protein. Here, red cabbage lends color, crunch, and a full plate of nutrients, including antioxidants and soluble fiber, which can help lower LDL cholesterol.

3 (6-ounce) boneless, skinless chicken breasts, cubed
Pinch salt
⅛ teaspoon white pepper
1 teaspoon toasted sesame oil
¼ cup low-fat mayonnaise
¼ cup low-sodium chicken broth
2 tablespoons fresh lemon juice
1 tablespoon low-sodium yellow mustard
2 tablespoons chopped fresh dill
4 cups shredded red cabbage
1 small yellow summer squash, sliced
1 small carrot, shredded
2 tablespoons sunflower seeds

1. Sprinkle the chicken with the salt and pepper.

2. Heat the sesame oil in a large nonstick skillet. Add the chicken and cook, stirring frequently, until lightly browned and cooked to 165°F when tested with a meat thermometer, about 5 to 7 minutes. Remove from the skillet and set aside.

3. In a large bowl, combine the mayonnaise, chicken broth, lemon juice, mustard, and dill and mix well.

4. Add the cabbage, squash, and carrot to the dressing in the bowl and toss.

5. Add the chicken to the salad and toss.

6. Sprinkle with the sunflower seeds and serve.

SUBSTITUTION TIP: You can substitute green cabbage for the red cabbage if you'd like. The vitamin A and vitamin C content will be reduced by about 30 percent, but the fiber content will stay the same. Add any of your favorite vegetables to this salad: try peas, green beans, or red bell pepper.

Per serving: Calories 256; Fat 9g (with 32% calories from fat); Saturated fat 2g; Monounsaturated fat 2g; Carbs 11g; Sodium 169mg; Dietary fiber 4g; Protein 32g; Cholesterol 76mg; Vitamin A 44% DV; Vitamin C 66% DV; Sugar 5g

Mixed Berry Chicken Salad

GLUTEN-FREE, NUT-FREE

SERVES 4 / **PREP TIME:** 20 minutes / **COOK TIME:** 8 minutes

Fresh berries are the perfect addition to chicken salads, especially when you want a festive, warm-weather meal that comes together quickly. Packed with four different kinds of sweet and tart berries, this salad is loaded with vitamins A and C. Berries are also high in fiber since they are full of little seeds.

4 (6-ounce) boneless, skinless chicken breasts, cubed
Pinch salt
⅛ teaspoon white pepper
2 teaspoons olive oil, divided
2 cups sliced strawberries
2 cups blueberries
1 cup blackberries
⅓ cup low-fat plain Greek yogurt
3 tablespoons fresh lime juice
2 tablespoons honey
1 teaspoon grated fresh lime zest
1 cup raspberries
4 cups mixed green lettuce

1. Sprinkle the chicken breasts with the salt and pepper.

2. Heat 1 teaspoon of the olive oil in a large nonstick skillet. Add the chicken and cook, stirring frequently, until lightly browned and cooked to 165°F when tested with a meat thermometer, about 5 to 7 minutes. Transfer to a clean plate.

3. In a large bowl, combine the strawberries, blueberries, and blackberries, and gently toss to mix.

4. In a small bowl, combine the yogurt, lime juice, honey, lime zest, and remaining 1 teaspoon olive oil, and mix well.

5. Add the chicken to the berry mixture, and drizzle the yogurt mixture over all the ingredients. Toss gently.

6. Top the chicken salad with the raspberries. Serve on a bed of the mixed green lettuce.

Per serving: Calories; 394 Fat 6g (with 14% calories from fat); Saturated fat 1g; Monounsaturated fat 2g; Carbs 42g; Sodium 138mg; Dietary fiber 8g; Protein 43g; Cholesterol 99mg; Vitamin A 58% DV; Vitamin C 170% DV; Sugar 25g

Hawaiian Chicken Stir-Fry

GLUTEN-FREE

SERVES 4 / **PREP TIME:** 20 minutes / **COOK TIME:** 10 minutes

Stir-frying is one of the quickest cooking methods on the planet. But all of the ingredients must be prepped before you begin because you can't stop to chop a pepper once you start cooking. This rich-tasting recipe is as colorful as it is flavorful. Serve the chicken by itself or atop brown rice or another fiber-filled grain.

1 (8-ounce) can crushed pineapple, undrained
⅓ cup water
2 tablespoons cornstarch
1 teaspoon brown sugar
1 teaspoon low-sodium tamari sauce
¼ teaspoon ground ginger
⅛ teaspoon cayenne pepper
2 tablespoons unsweetened shredded coconut
2 tablespoons chopped macadamia nuts
2 teaspoons olive oil
1 onion, chopped
1 red bell pepper, seeded and chopped
3 (6-ounce) boneless, skinless chicken breasts, cubed

1. In a medium bowl, combine the pineapple, water, cornstarch, brown sugar, tamari, ginger, and cayenne pepper, and mix well. Set aside.

2. Place a large nonstick skillet or wok over medium heat. Add the coconut and macadamia nuts, and toast for 1 to 2 minutes, stirring constantly, until fragrant. Remove from the skillet and set aside.

3. Add the olive oil to the skillet and heat over medium-high heat. Add the onion and red bell pepper, and stir-fry for 2 to 3 minutes or until

almost tender.

4. Add the chicken to the wok, and stir-fry for 3 to 4 minutes or until lightly browned.

5. Stir the sauce, add to the skillet, and stir fry for 1 to 2 minutes longer until the sauce thickens and the chicken registers at 165°F when tested with a meat thermometer.

6. Serve immediately, topped with the toasted coconut and macadamia nuts.

Per serving: Calories 301; Fat 12g (with 36% calories from fat); Saturated fat 4g; Monounsaturated fat 6g; Carbs 18g; Sodium 131mg; Dietary fiber 3g; Protein 31g; Cholesterol 73mg; Vitamin A 20% DV; Vitamin C 77% DV; Sugar 11g

Pineapple Curried Chicken

GLUTEN-FREE, NUT-FREE

SERVES 4 / **PREP TIME:** 15 minutes / **COOK TIME:** 15 minutes

Curry powder is an excellent spice to use with mild and tender chicken. Pineapple adds sweetness along with a good dose of fiber, which can help lower cholesterol levels. The addition of cayenne pepper means this dish brings some heat! Serve over hot cooked brown rice, farro, or quinoa for a filling meal.

3 (6-ounce) boneless, skinless chicken breasts, cubed

2 teaspoons curry powder

2 tablespoons cornstarch

⅛ teaspoon cayenne pepper

1 teaspoon olive oil

2 shallots, minced

3 cloves garlic, minced

1 (16-ounce) can pineapple chunks, drained, reserving juice

2 teaspoons yellow curry paste (optional)

⅓ cup reserved pineapple juice

1 tablespoon fresh lemon juice

3 tablespoons plain nonfat Greek yogurt

1. In a medium bowl, toss the chicken breast cubes with the curry powder, cornstarch, and cayenne pepper, and set aside.

2. In a large nonstick skillet, heat the olive oil over medium heat.

3. Add the shallots and garlic, and cook for 2 minutes, stirring frequently.

4. Add the coated chicken cubes. Cook and stir for 5 to 6 minutes or until the chicken starts to brown.

5. Add the pineapple chunks, yellow curry paste (if using), reserved pineapple juice, and lemon juice to the skillet and bring to a simmer.

6. Simmer for 3 to 4 minutes or until the chicken is cooked to 165°F when tested with a meat thermometer. Stir in the yogurt and serve hot.

INGREDIENT TIP: Curry pastes are a concentrated and strong form of curry. They come in red, yellow, and green. Red curry paste is the hottest, green is a little bit milder, and yellow is mild and creamy. Choose the spice level you like for this recipe, or leave it out altogether if you prefer a milder dish.

Per serving: Calories 260; Fat 3g (with 10% calories from fat); Saturated fat 1g; Monounsaturated fat 1g; Carbs 24g; Sodium 93mg; Dietary fiber 1g; Protein 31g; Cholesterol 72mg; Vitamin A 3% DV; Vitamin C 37% DV; Sugar 15g

Basil Chicken Meatballs

GLUTEN-FREE, NUT-FREE

MAKES 20 meatballs (serves 4) / **PREP TIME:** 15 minutes / **COOK TIME:** 10 minutes

Chicken meatballs are a nice change of pace from regular beef meatballs. And they are lower in fat and cholesterol. These tender little meatballs are flavored with chives and basil. They are delicious coated in spaghetti sauce or served up plain as appetizers.

1 egg white
⅓ cup gluten-free (or whole-wheat) bread crumbs
½ cup low-sodium chicken broth, divided
1 tablespoon fresh lemon juice
1 tablespoon freeze-dried chopped chives
3 tablespoons minced fresh basil leaves
⅛ teaspoon garlic powder
Pinch salt
Pinch black pepper
¾ pound ground white chicken breast meat

1. In a medium bowl, combine the egg white, bread crumbs, 2 tablespoons of the chicken broth, lemon juice, chives, basil, garlic powder, salt, and pepper, and mix well.

2. Add the ground chicken and mix gently but thoroughly until combined.

3. Form into 20 meatballs, about 1 inch in diameter.

4. Heat the remaining 6 tablespoons of the chicken broth in a large nonstick skillet over medium-high heat.

5. Gently add the chicken meatballs in a single layer. Let cook for 5 minutes, then carefully turn and cook another 3 minutes.

6. Lower the heat as the broth reduces, and continue cooking the meatballs, gently shaking the pan occasionally, until the broth has mostly evaporated and the meatballs are browned and cooked to 165°F as tested with a meat thermometer, another 2 to 3 minutes.

COOKING TIP: All recipes made with chicken should be cooked to a minimum internal temperature of 165°F (when tested with a meat thermometer) for food safety reasons. Handle chicken carefully to avoid cross-contamination between the raw meat and other foods, especially those that are eaten uncooked.

Per serving: Calories 130; Fat 3g (with 21% calories from fat); Saturated fat 1g; Monounsaturated fat 0g; Carbs 5g; Sodium 162mg; Dietary fiber 1g; Protein 20g; Cholesterol 52mg; Vitamin A 4% DV; Vitamin C 3% DV; Sugar 0g

Mustard-Roasted Almond Chicken Tenders

GLUTEN-FREE

SERVES 4 / **PREP TIME:** 15 minutes / **COOK TIME:** 15 minutes

Not your typical kids' finger food, these chicken tenders have a flavorful mustard profile and are an ideal choice for a quick-cooking meal. Almonds are rich in flavor and can help lower cholesterol levels.

¼ **cup low-sodium yellow mustard**
2 **teaspoons yellow mustard seed**
¼ **teaspoon dry mustard**
⅛ **teaspoon garlic powder**
1 **egg white**
2 **tablespoons fresh lemon juice**
¼ **cup almond flour**
¼ **cup ground almonds**
1 **pound chicken tenders**

1. Preheat the oven to 400°F. Place a wire rack on a baking sheet.

2. In a shallow bowl, combine the yellow mustard, mustard seed, ground mustard, garlic powder, egg white, and lemon juice, and whisk well.

3. To a plate or shallow bowl, add the almond flour and ground almonds, and combine.

4. Dip the chicken tenders into the mustard-egg mixture, then into the almond mixture to coat. Place each tender on the rack on the baking pan as you work.

5. Bake the chicken for 12 to 15 minutes or until a meat thermometer registers 165°F. Serve immediately.

DID YOU KNOW? Chicken tenders are actually the tenderloin, a muscle underneath the chicken breast.

Per serving: Calories 166; Fat 4g (with 22% calories from fat); Saturated fat 0g; Monounsaturated fat 1g; Carbs 2g; Sodium 264mg; Dietary fiber 1g; Protein 29g; Cholesterol 66mg; Vitamin A 1% DV; Vitamin C 9% DV; Sugar 1g

Nutty Coconut Chicken with Fruit Sauce

GLUTEN-FREE

SERVES 4 / **PREP TIME:** 15 minutes / **COOK TIME:** 15 minutes

The combination of coconut and nuts creates a satisfying crunchy crust on these tender chicken strips. And while the fruit sauce is rich, tart, and sweet, it's also healthy—the perfect complement.

¼ cup ground almonds
⅓ cup unsweetened flaked coconut
¼ cup coconut flour
Pinch salt
⅛ teaspoon white pepper
1 egg white
1 (16-ounce) package chicken tenders
1 cup sliced strawberries
1 cup raspberries
⅓ cup unsweetened white grape juice
1 tablespoon lemon juice
½ teaspoon dried thyme leaves
⅓ cup dried cherries

1. Preheat the oven to 400°F. Place a wire rack on a baking sheet.

2. In a shallow plate, combine the ground almonds, flaked coconut, coconut flour, salt, and white pepper, and mix well.

3. In a shallow bowl, beat the egg white just until foamy.

4. Dip the chicken tenders into the egg white, then into the almond mixture to coat. Place on the wire rack as you work.

5. Bake the chicken tenders for 14 to 16 minutes or until the chicken is cooked to 165°F when tested with a meat thermometer.

6. While the chicken is baking, in a food processor or blender, combine the strawberries, raspberries, grape juice, lemon juice, and thyme leaves and process or blend until smooth.

7. Pour the mixture into a small saucepan, and add the dried cherries. Bring to a simmer over medium heat. Simmer for 3 minutes, then remove the pan from the heat and set aside.

8. Serve the chicken with the warm fruit sauce.

Per serving: Calories 281; Fat 8g (with 26% calories from fat); Saturated fat 3g; Monounsaturated fat 2g; Carbs 23g; Sodium 124mg; Dietary fiber 7g; Protein 30g; Cholesterol 64mg; Vitamin A 11% DV; Vitamin C 64% DV; Sugar 14g

"Butter" Chicken

GLUTEN-FREE, NUT-FREE

SERVES 4 / **PREP TIME:** 15 minutes / **COOK TIME:** 12 minutes

The classic Indian recipe for butter chicken is made with dairy, but you don't have to use butter to create a dish with the same delicious flavor profile. Curry powder adds lots of depth and provides the heart-healthy compound curcumin. Butter chicken is especially good with cooked bulgur, brown rice, or quinoa.

4 (6-ounce) boneless, skinless chicken breasts, cubed
2 tablespoons fresh lemon juice
2 teaspoons curry powder
1 teaspoon chili powder
⅛ teaspoon black pepper
2 teaspoons olive oil
1 onion, chopped
4 cloves garlic, minced
½ cup low-fat coconut milk
½ cup low-fat plain Greek yogurt
2 tablespoons no-salt-added tomato paste
1 tablespoon cornstarch

1. In a large bowl, combine the chicken with the lemon juice, curry powder, chili powder, and black pepper, and mix with your hands, rubbing the spices into the chicken. Set aside.

2. In a large nonstick skillet, heat the olive oil over medium heat.

3. Add the onion and garlic, and sauté for 4 to 5 minutes, until tender.

4. Add the chicken and sauté, stirring frequently, until the chicken starts to brown, about 4 minutes.

5. Meanwhile, in a small bowl, combine the coconut milk, yogurt, tomato paste, and cornstarch, and mix well with a whisk.

6. Add the coconut milk mixture to the skillet. Simmer 4 to 5 minutes or until the sauce is thickened and the chicken registers 165°F on a meat thermometer. Serve hot.

Per serving: Calories 308; Fat 8g (with 23% calories from fat); Saturated fat 3g; Monounsaturated fat 2g; Carbs 14g; Sodium 144mg; Dietary fiber 3g; Protein 42g; Cholesterol 99mg; Vitamin A 7% DV; Vitamin C 21% DV; Sugar 8g

Moroccan Chicken

GLUTEN-FREE, NUT-FREE

SERVES 4 / **PREP TIME:** 15 minutes / **COOK TIME:** 15 minutes

Moroccan cuisine uses delightfully fragrant ingredients, including the spices cinnamon, cumin, turmeric, ginger, paprika, and anise. The addition of garlic, sugar snap peas, and carrots in this recipe bumps up the fiber content.

3 (4-ounce) boneless, skinless chicken thighs, cubed
1 teaspoon smoked paprika
½ teaspoon ground cinnamon
½ teaspoon ground cumin
⅛ teaspoon ground ginger
1 cup low-sodium chicken broth
2 tablespoons fresh lemon juice
1 tablespoon cornstarch
1 teaspoon olive oil
1 onion, chopped
3 cloves garlic, minced
2 cups sugar snap peas
1 cup shredded carrots

1. Put the cubed chicken in a medium bowl. Sprinkle with the paprika, cinnamon, cumin, and ginger, and work the spices into the meat. Set aside.

2. In a small bowl, combine the chicken broth, lemon juice, and cornstarch and mix well. Set aside.

3. Heat the olive oil in a large nonstick skillet over medium-high heat. Add the chicken thighs, and sauté for 5 minutes or until the chicken starts to brown. Remove the chicken from the pan and set aside.

4. Add the onion and garlic to the skillet, and sauté for 3 minutes.

5. Add the sugar snap peas and carrots to the skillet and sauté for 2 minutes.

6. Return the chicken to the skillet and stir. Add the chicken broth mixture, bring to a simmer, and turn down the heat to low. Simmer 3 to 4 minutes or until the sauce thickens, the vegetables are tender, and the chicken is cooked to 165°F on a meat thermometer. Serve hot.

SUBSTITUTION TIP: You could substitute 4 (6-ounce) chicken breasts for the chicken thighs in this recipe to get more meat per serving. The calories would increase to 262, but the fat would drop to 21 percent calories. You would also lose 1 gram of saturated fat, but the sodium level would increase to 400 mg per serving.

Per serving: Calories 165; Fat 5g (with 27% calories from fat); Saturated fat 1g; Monounsaturated fat 3g; Carbs 11g; Sodium 112mg; Dietary fiber 3g; Protein 18g; Cholesterol 70mg; Vitamin A 267% DV; Vitamin C 67% DV; Sugar 4g

Piri Piri Chicken

GLUTEN-FREE, NUT-FREE

SERVES 4 / **PREP TIME:** 15 minutes / **COOK TIME:** 15 minutes

Piri Piri is a very hot and spicy sauce from Portugal that is made with red chile peppers. The chicken is typically grilled and basted with the sauce. This one-dish adaptation has great smoky, spicy flavor but is easier to make.

3 (6-ounce) boneless, skinless chicken breasts, cubed
2 tablespoons lemon juice
1 teaspoon smoked paprika
½ teaspoon cayenne pepper
Pinch salt
2 teaspoons chili powder
1 teaspoon olive oil
1 onion, chopped
4 cloves garlic, minced
1 red bell pepper, chopped
1 red chile pepper, such as chile de arbol, seeded and minced
2 tablespoons Piri Piri sauce
1 cup low-sodium chicken broth
1 tablespoon cornstarch

1. Place the chicken breasts in a medium bowl and drizzle with the lemon juice.

2. Sprinkle the chicken with the smoked paprika, cayenne pepper, salt, and chili powder. Work the spices into the chicken with your hands and set aside.

3. In a large nonstick skillet, heat the olive oil over medium heat.

4. Add the chicken to the skillet. Cook, stirring frequently, until the chicken is lightly browned, about 4 minutes. Transfer the chicken to a clean plate.

5. Add the onion, garlic, red bell pepper, red chile pepper, and Piri Piri sauce to the skillet stir. Sauté 3 to 4 minutes or until the vegetables are crisp-tender. Return the chicken to the skillet.

6. In a small bowl, combine the chicken broth and cornstarch and mix with a whisk. Stir into the chicken mixture.

7. Simmer 3 to 4 minutes or until the chicken is cooked to 165°F when tested with a meat thermometer, and the sauce is thickened. Serve immediately.

SUBSTITUTION TIP: Piri Piri sauce can be very high in sodium, so check the package label before you buy. You can substitute Tabasco sauce or any hot sauce, such as Buffalo sauce, for the Piri Piri sauce if you can't find it in your grocery store.

Per serving: Calories 209; Fat 5g (with 22% calories from fat); Saturated fat 1g; Monounsaturated fat 2g; Carbs 10g; Sodium 210mg; Dietary fiber 2g; Protein 31g; Cholesterol 78mg; Vitamin A 32% DV; Vitamin C 93% DV; Sugar 4g

Mini Turkey Meatloaves

GLUTEN-FREE, NUT-FREE

SERVES 4 / **PREP TIME:** 10 minutes / **COOK TIME:** 20 minutes

Meatloaf usually takes a long time to cook. But we're making mini meatloaves here, which kids love and which reduces the cooking time considerably. Oats add soluble fiber and texture to this simple recipe.

⅓ cup old-fashioned rolled oats
2 scallions, finely chopped
1 egg
3 tablespoons no-salt-added tomato paste, divided
2 teaspoons olive oil
Pinch salt
⅛ teaspoon black pepper
½ teaspoon dried ground leaves
16 ounces 99% lean ground white turkey
2 tablespoons low-sodium mustard
1 tablespoon water

1. Preheat the oven to 450°F. Line a baking sheet with aluminum foil.

2. In a large bowl, combine the oats, scallions, egg, 2 tablespoons of the tomato paste, olive oil, salt, pepper, and marjoram, and mix well.

3. Add the ground turkey, and mix gently with your hands until well combined.

4. Divide the mixture into fourths and shape into mini loaves. Place on the prepared baking sheet.

5. In a small bowl, combine the remaining 1 tablespoon tomato paste, the mustard, and water and mix well. Brush over the mini

meatloaves.

6. Bake for 18 to 22 minutes or until the meatloaves register 165°F on a meat thermometer.

Per serving: Calories 205; Fat 5g (with 21% calories from fat); Saturated fat 1g; Monounsaturated fat 0g; Carbs 8g; Sodium 252mg; Dietary fiber 1g; Protein 30g; Cholesterol 111mg; Vitamin A 4% DV; Vitamin C 4% DV; Sugar 1g

Grilled Turkey and Veggie Kabobs

GLUTEN-FREE, NUT-FREE

SERVES 4 / **PREP TIME:** 20 minutes / **COOK TIME:** 10 minutes

Kabobs are a fun and efficient way to work more heart-healthy veggies into your diet. Using the grill adds a rich, smoky flavor to this simple recipe—just make sure your grill rack is very clean before you cook! You should have 8 (10-inch) metal kebob skewers for this recipe.

1 pound turkey tenderloin
Pinch salt
⅛ teaspoon cayenne pepper
1 yellow summer squash, cut into ½-inch slices
1 orange bell pepper, seeded and cut into 1-inch cubes
1 red bell pepper, seeded and cut into 1-inch cubes
3 scallions, cut into 2-inch pieces
¼ cup apple jelly
2 tablespoons fresh lemon juice
1 tablespoon butter
1 tablespoon low-sodium mustard
1 teaspoon dried oregano leaves

1. Prepare and preheat the grill to medium heat.

2. Cut the turkey into 1-inch cubes, put on a plate, and sprinkle with the salt and cayenne pepper.

3. Thread the turkey cubes, alternating with the squash, orange bell pepper, red bell pepper, and scallion, onto kabob skewers.

4. In a small saucepan, combine the apple jelly, lemon juice, and butter. Heat over low heat until the apple jelly melts and the

mixture is smooth, about 2 minutes. Stir in the mustard and oregano.

5. Place the kabobs on the hot grill and brush with some of the apple jelly mixture. Cover and grill for 4 minutes.

6. Uncover, turn the kabobs, and brush with more of the apple jelly mixture. Cover and grill for 3 minutes.

7. Uncover the grill and turn the kabobs, brushing with the remaining apple jelly mixture, and cook until the turkey registers 165°F on a meat thermometer, 2 to 3 minutes longer. Use all of the apple jelly mixture; if any is left, discard it.

INGREDIENT TIP: Turkey tenderloin comes in several different varieties and flavors. It is very low in fat and quick-cooking, but you have to pay attention when you shop. For these recipes, choose the plain variety. Other varieties, including teriyaki and smoked, can be very high in sodium and sugar.

Per serving: Calories 232; Fat 5g (with 19% calories from fat); Saturated fat 2g; Monounsaturated fat 0g; Carbs 21g; Sodium 194mg; Dietary fiber 2g; Protein 30g; Cholesterol 53mg; Vitamin A 34% DV; Vitamin C 145% DV; Sugar 15g

Lemon Tarragon Turkey Medallions

GLUTEN-FREE, NUT-FREE

SERVES 4 / **PREP TIME:** 15 minutes / **COOK TIME:** 10 minutes

Turkey medallions are simply rounds of turkey that are cut from the tenderloin. Turkey tenderloin cooks up quickly, and as the name reveals, it's a tender and delicious cut. In this preparation it gets a Mediterranean flair, seasoned with fresh lemon and tarragon.

1 pound turkey tenderloin
Pinch salt
⅛ teaspoon lemon pepper
2 tablespoons cornstarch
1 teaspoon dried tarragon leaves
¼ cup fresh lemon juice
½ cup low-sodium chicken stock
1 teaspoon grated fresh lemon zest
2 teaspoons olive oil

1. Cut the turkey tenderloin crosswise into ½-inch slices. Sprinkle with the salt and lemon pepper.

2. In a small bowl, combine the cornstarch, tarragon, lemon juice, chicken stock, and lemon zest, and mix well.

3. Heat the olive oil in a large nonstick skillet over medium heat.

4. Add the turkey tenderloins. Cook for 2 minutes, and then turn and cook for another 2 minutes.

5. Add the lemon juice mixture to the skillet. Cook, stirring frequently, until the sauce boils and thickens and the turkey is cooked to 165°F on a meat thermometer. Serve immediately.

Per serving: Calories 169; Fat 3g (with 16% calories from fat); Saturated fat 1g; Monounsaturated fat 2g; Carbs 5g; Sodium 77mg; Dietary fiber 0g; Protein 29g; Cholesterol 70mg; Vitamin A 0% DV; Vitamin C 12% DV; Sugar 0g

Tandoori Turkey Pizzas

NUT-FREE

SERVES 4 / **PREP TIME:** 12 minutes / **COOK TIME:** 18 minutes

Tandoori is an Indian style of cooking in a special clay oven. This dish features the aromatic spices used in Indian cooking, including curry powder, cumin, and garlic. Using whole-wheat pita bread for the pizza crust adds a dose of heart-healthy fiber.

4 (6½-inch) whole-wheat pita breads
1 teaspoon olive oil
1 onion, chopped
4 cloves garlic, minced
½ pound ground turkey
1 (8-ounce) can no-salt-added tomato sauce
2 teaspoons curry powder
½ teaspoon smoked paprika
¼ teaspoon ground cumin
⅛ teaspoon cayenne pepper
¼ cup crumbled feta cheese
3 tablespoons low-fat plain Greek yogurt

1. Preheat the oven to 425°F. Place the pita breads on a baking sheet lined with aluminum foil and set aside.

2. In a large skillet, heat the olive oil over medium heat. Add the onion and garlic and cook, stirring frequently, for 2 minutes.

3. Add the ground turkey and sauté, breaking up the meat. Cook for 5 minutes or until the turkey is no longer pink.

4. Add the tomato sauce, curry powder, paprika, cumin, and cayenne pepper to the sauce and bring to a simmer. Simmer over low heat for 1 minute.

5. Top the pita "pizzas" evenly with the turkey mixture. Sprinkle each with the feta cheese.

6. Bake for 10 to 12 minutes or until the pizzas are hot. Drizzle each pizza with the yogurt and serve immediately.

SUBSTITUTION TIP: If you cannot eat gluten, you can substitute gluten-free pita for the whole-wheat pita in this recipe. They are usually sold frozen; thaw according to the package directions. The fiber content of the recipe may decrease slightly.

Per serving: Calories 308; Fat 6g (with 18% calories from fat); Saturated fat 2g; Monounsaturated fat 1g; Carbs 43g; Sodium 779mg; Dietary fiber 7g; Protein 24g; Cholesterol 40mg; Vitamin A 9% DV; Vitamin C 16% DV; Sugar 5g

Turkey Tacos Verde

GLUTEN-FREE, NUT-FREE

MAKES 8 tacos (serves 4) / **PREP TIME:** 15 minutes / **COOK TIME:** 13 minutes

The word *verde* in Spanish means green. In this recipe you'll use green tomatillos instead of cherry or plum tomatoes. This recipe also uses jalapeño peppers and green bell pepper for a lot of flavor and fiber—and minimal fat. And a lovely color!

1 teaspoon olive oil
1 pound 99% lean ground white turkey
1 onion, chopped
3 cloves garlic, minced
10 tomatillos, husk removed, rinsed and chopped
2 jalapeño peppers, seeded and minced
½ cup low-sodium salsa verde
8 corn tortillas, warmed
½ cup low-fat plain Greek yogurt
2 tablespoons chopped fresh cilantro
2 scallions, minced
2 cups mixed salad greens

1. In a large nonstick skillet, heat the olive oil over medium heat.

2. Add the ground turkey, onion, and garlic and stir to break up the meat.

3. Sauté the mixture until the turkey is cooked through, about 5 to 6 minutes.

4. Add the tomatillos and jalapeño peppers and stir for 3 to 4 minutes. Then add the salsa verde and stir.

5. Meanwhile, combine the yogurt, cilantro, and scallions in a small bowl

6. Assemble the tacos starting with the tortillas, turkey mixture, yogurt mixture, and top with the salad greens. Serve immediately.

INGREDIENT TIP: Tomatillos are a type of fruit used in Mexican cooking that are similar to a tomato. They are encased in a husk and are covered in a sticky substance. You can find them in most grocery stores; if not, ask your grocer; they can order them. Peel off the husk and rinse the tomatillos before you chop them.

Per serving: Calories 338; Fat 6g (with 16% calories from fat); Saturated fat 1g; Monounsaturated fat 3g; Carbs 35g; Sodium 295mg; Dietary fiber 6g; Protein 36g; Cholesterol 71mg; Vitamin A 50% DV; Vitamin C 56% DV; Sugar 4g

Korean Beef Bowl

CHAPTER FIVE

Beef and Pork

Beef and Broccoli

Stir-Fried Crispy Orange Beef

Korean Beef Bowl

Beef Burrito Skillet

Beef and Avocado Quesadillas

Lemon Garlic Flank Steak Wraps

Teriyaki Beef Skewers

Beef and Mushroom Burger

Mini Lasagna Cups

Spinach and Kale Salad with Spicy Pork

Chile Pork with Soba Noodles

Pork and Fennel Stir Fry

Lemon Basil Pork Medallions

Pepper Pot

Pork Goulash

Beef and Broccoli

NUT-FREE

SERVES 4 / **PREP TIME:** 15 minutes / **COOK TIME:** 10 minutes

The classic restaurant-style stir-fry recipe is typically high in fat and sodium. This reworked recipe uses less beef and adds more fibrous veggies and seasonings for a satisfying low-fat dinner.

½ **pound top sirloin steak**
⅛ **teaspoon cayenne pepper**
¼ **teaspoon ground ginger**
1¼ **cups low-sodium beef broth**
1 **tablespoon honey**
2 **tablespoons cornstarch**
1 **teaspoon hoisin sauce**
1 **teaspoon low-sodium soy sauce**
1 **teaspoon olive oil**
1 **onion, chopped**
3 **cloves garlic, minced**
3 **cups broccoli florets**

1. Trim any visible fat from the steak. Cut the steak into ½-inch strips. Place in a bowl, sprinkle with the cayenne pepper and ginger, and toss. Set aside.

2. In a small bowl, thoroughly combine the beef broth, honey, cornstarch, hoisin sauce, and soy sauce. Set aside.

3. In a large nonstick skillet or wok, heat the olive oil over medium-high heat.

4. Add the steak strips in a single layer, and cook for 1 minute. Turn the steak and cook for 1 minute longer. Transfer the steak to a plate.

5. Add the onion and garlic to the skillet, and stir-fry for 2 minutes.

6. Add the broccoli, and stir-fry for 2 minutes.

7. Add the broth mixture and bring to a simmer. Simmer for 1 to 2 minutes or until the sauce has thickened.

8. Return the beef to the skillet, and stir-fry for 1 minute. Serve immediately.

INGREDIENT TIP: You can buy precut broccoli florets at the supermarket to save time, or you can cut the florets off a full broccoli stalk. Look where the florets start to branch out; cut them from the main stem at this point. You can use the stem too. Just peel it and cut into 1-inch slices.

Per serving: Calories 204; Fat 9g (with 40% calories from fat); Saturated fat 3g; Monounsaturated fat 4g; Carbs 17g; Sodium 141mg; Dietary fiber 2g; Protein 13g; Cholesterol 27mg; Vitamin A 9% DV; Vitamin C 105% DV; Sugar 7g

Stir-Fried Crispy Orange Beef

NUT-FREE

SERVES 4 / **PREP TIME:** 18 minutes / **COOK TIME:** 12 minutes

Crispy beef is a mouthwatering Chinese food classic. Traditionally, the beef is coated in cornstarch and deep fried until crispy. In this low-fat makeover, you cut the beef into thin strips, coat them in rice flour, and sauté in a fraction of the oil in batches until crisp. Serve over hot cooked brown rice or bulgur.

½ cup low-sodium beef broth, divided

3 tablespoons orange juice

1 teaspoon fresh orange zest

1 teaspoon low-sodium soy sauce

1 teaspoon Thai chili paste

2 tablespoons rice flour or cornstarch, divided

½ pound top round steak

1 teaspoon paprika

⅛ teaspoon cayenne pepper

1 teaspoon olive oil

3 scallions, chopped

2 cups snow pea pods

1 red bell pepper, seeded and chopped

1 carrot, grated

1. In a small bowl, combine all but 1 tablespoon of the beef broth, the orange juice, orange zest, soy sauce, Thai chili paste, and 1 tablespoon of the rice flour or cornstarch, and mix well. Set aside.

2. Trim off the fat from the steak and discard. Slice into thin strips and put in a medium bowl. Add the remaining 1 tablespoon rice flour or cornstarch, the paprika, and cayenne pepper to the beef and toss to coat.

3. Heat ½ teaspoon of the olive oil in a nonstick skillet or wok over high heat.

4. Add half the beef strips in a single layer. Let them cook for 2 minutes, then turn and cook for 2 to 3 minutes or until the beef is crisp. Remove the beef to a clean plate.

5. Repeat with remaining ½ teaspoon olive oil and beef strips. Remove the beef to the plate.

6. Reduce the heat to medium high. Add reserved 1 tablespoon beef broth to the skillet, then add the scallions, pea pods, and carrots. Stir-fry for 2 to 3 minutes, or until the vegetables are crisp-tender.

7. Add the orange–beef broth mixture to the skillet and stir-fry for 1 to 2 minutes or until the sauce has thickened slightly. Add the beef strips, and stir-fry for 1 minute.

SUBSTITUTION TIP: The leanest cuts of beef for low-fat recipes include top round, eye of round, top sirloin, flap steak, and sirloin tip steak. You can use any of them in this recipe; just trim off and discard visible fat before you prepare the meat.

Per serving: Calories 175; Fat 4g (with 21% calories from fat); Saturated fat 1g; Monounsaturated fat 0g; Carbs 16g; Sodium 194mg; Dietary fiber 4g; Protein 17g; Cholesterol 38mg; Vitamin A 20% DV; Vitamin C 75% DV; Sugar 7g

Korean Beef Bowl

NUT-FREE

SERVES 4 / **PREP TIME:** 20 minutes / **COOK TIME:** 10 minutes

You won't miss the classic recipe for this dish when you try this makeover. It includes filling, fiber-rich quick-cooking veggies in a decadent spicy-sweet sauce. It's heart-healthy and a real crowd-pleaser!

½ cup low-sodium beef broth

2 teaspoons low-sodium soy sauce

2 teaspoons cornstarch

1 teaspoon honey

⅛ teaspoon Tabasco sauce

12 ounces 98% lean ground beef

5 scallions, chopped

5 cloves garlic, minced

1 tablespoon grated peeled fresh ginger root

1 cup frozen edamame, thawed and shelled (see Ingredient Tip)

1 yellow bell pepper, seeded and chopped

1 cup shredded carrot

2 cups fresh baby spinach leaves

1. In a small bowl, add the beef broth, soy sauce, cornstarch, honey, and Tabasco sauce, and whisk to combine. Set aside.

2. In a large nonstick skillet, cook the ground beef, scallions, garlic, and ginger root, stirring to break up the beef, until the beef is browned, about 4 minutes. Drain off the fat if necessary.

3. Add the shelled edamame, bell pepper, and carrot to the skillet, and stir-fry for 3 to 4 minutes or until the vegetables are crisp-tender.

4. Add the beef broth mixture, and stir-fry 2 minutes or until the sauce is thickened.

5. Stir in the spinach leaves. Cover and let rest for 1 minute until the spinach wilts. Serve immediately.

Per serving: Calories 220; Fat 6g (with 25% calories from fat); Saturated fat 2g; Monounsaturated fat 0g; Carbs 17g; Sodium 295mg; Dietary fiber 5g; Protein 27g; Cholesterol 35mg; Vitamin A 43% DV; Vitamin C 160% DV; Sugar 4g

Beef Burrito Skillet

GLUTEN-FREE, NUT-FREE

SERVES 4 / **PREP TIME:** 15 minutes / **COOK TIME:** 15 minutes

Beef burritos are a Mexican classic, combining beans, cheese, and beef, rolled up in tortillas. This casserole version is made on the stovetop and adds lots of veggies for more nutrition and less fat.

¾ pound extra-lean ground beef
1 onion, chopped
4 cloves garlic, minced
1 jalapeño pepper, seeded and minced
1 tablespoon chili powder
½ teaspoon cumin
1 (16-ounce) can no-salt-added pinto beans, rinsed and drained
1 tomato, chopped
1 cup frozen corn, thawed
½ cup low-sodium salsa
3 corn tortillas, cut into 1-inch strips
2 tablespoons crumbled cotija cheese
¼ cup low-fat sour cream

1. In a large skillet, sauté the ground beef, onion, garlic, and jalapeño pepper, stirring to break up the meat, until the beef is browned, about 5 to 7 minutes.

2. Add the chili powder and cumin, and stir.

3. Add in the pinto beans, tomato, corn, and salsa, and bring to a simmer. Simmer for 5 minutes, stirring occasionally.

4. Stir in the corn tortillas and cook for 3 to 4 minutes. Top with the cheese and sour cream, and serve.

Per serving: Calories 403; Fat 10g (with 23% calories from fat); Saturated fat 4g; Monounsaturated fat 0g; Carbs 54g; Sodium 215mg; Dietary fiber 14g; Protein 32g; Cholesterol 59mg; Vitamin A 10% DV; Vitamin C 37% DV; Sugar 7g

Beef and Avocado Quesadillas

NUT-FREE

SERVES 4 / **PREP TIME:** 10 minutes / **COOK TIME:** 10 minutes

Quesadillas make the ideal quick meal or snack—and prep is made even easier if you purchase presliced and preshredded vegetables. With the addition of avocado, you get a nice serving of heart-healthy monounsaturated fat.

½ **pound 98% lean ground beef**
1 **small onion, chopped**
3 **cloves garlic, minced**
8 **medium mushrooms, sliced**
1 **cup shredded carrot**
½ **cup low-sodium salsa**
½ **cup low-fat mozzarella cheese**
½ **avocado, peeled and diced**
4 **whole-wheat flour tortillas**

1. In a large nonstick skillet, sauté the ground beef, onion, garlic, mushrooms, and carrot, stirring to break up the meat, until the meat is browned and fully cooked, about 5 to 6 minutes. Drain if necessary.

2. Transfer the beef mixture to a medium bowl and stir in the salsa.

3. Place the tortillas on the work surface. Divide the meat mixture among them, placing the meat on half of the tortilla. Top with the cheese and avocado. Fold the tortillas over and press gently into a quesadilla.

4. Rinse and dry the nonstick skillet.

5. One at a time, place the quesadillas into the skillet over medium heat, and cook for 2 to 3 minutes on each side. Cut the quesadillas in

half and serve immediately.

SUBSTITUTION TIP: To make these quesadillas gluten-free, use corn tortillas in place of the whole-wheat tortillas. You'll need eight corn tortillas because they are smaller than the wheat variety. Assemble and cook them the same way.

Per serving: Calories 237; Fat 9g (with 34% calories from fat); Saturated fat 3g; Monounsaturated fat 4g; Carbs 22g; Sodium 344mg; Dietary fiber 5g; Protein 20g; Cholesterol 44mg; Vitamin A 96% DV; Vitamin C 11% DV; Sugar 4g

Lemon Garlic Flank Steak Wraps

NUT-FREE

SERVES 4 / **PREP TIME:** 15 minutes / **COOK TIME:** 15 minutes

Flank steak is a lean cut of beef, so it's a heart-healthy choice. To be wonderfully tender, flank steak must be sliced across the grain. The abundance of fresh, raw vegetables in this dish contrasts well with the seasoned steak slices. Serve this dish for a decadent lunch.

½ pound flank steak
⅛ teaspoon garlic powder
Pinch salt
⅛ teaspoon lemon pepper
3 tablespoons fresh lemon juice
1 tablespoon orange juice
1 red bell pepper, seeded and sliced
1 cucumber, sliced
3 stalks celery, sliced
2 cups fresh baby spinach
4 (8-inch) whole-wheat flour tortillas

1. In a shallow bowl, sprinkle the flank steak with the garlic powder, salt, and lemon pepper. Drizzle all over with the lemon juice and orange juice and let stand for 10 minutes while you prepare the rest of the ingredients.

2. Heat a grill pan or nonstick skillet over medium-high heat. Add the steak, and cook 5 to 6 minutes per side, turning once, until cooked to at least 145°F on a meat thermometer.

3. Remove the steak from the grill and let rest for 2 minutes. Cut the steak across the grain into thin slices.

4. Divide the steak, vegetables, and spinach, among the 4 tortillas. Roll up, tucking in the ends, cut in half, and serve.

Per serving: Calories 292; Fat 9g (with 28% calories from fat); Saturated fat 4g; Monounsaturated fat 0g; Carbs 31g; Sodium 513mg; Dietary fiber 2g; Protein 21g; Cholesterol 40mg; Vitamin A 40% DV; Vitamin C 87% DV; Sugar 4g

Teriyaki Beef Skewers

NUT-FREE

SERVES 4 / **PREP TIME:** 15 minutes / **COOK TIME:** 15 minutes

Classic teriyaki is delicious—but high in salt. This low-fat, low-sodium version keeps the flavor and adds vegetables.

¾ pound top sirloin steak, cut into 1-inch cubes
¼ cup low-sodium beef broth
2 tablespoons rice wine vinegar
2 tablespoons fresh lemon juice
2 tablespoons honey
1 teaspoon toasted sesame oil
1 teaspoon hoisin sauce
¼ teaspoon garlic powder
¼ teaspoon ground ginger
2 yellow summer squash, cut into ½-inch slices
12 medium mushrooms, halved
2 red bell peppers, cut into ½-inch strips

1. Prepare and preheat the grill to medium heat.

2. Trim any visible fat from the steak and discard, and cut the steak into 1-inch cubes. Put the steak in a medium bowl and add the beef broth, vinegar, lemon juice, honey, sesame oil, hoisin sauce, garlic powder, and ground ginger, and mix well.

3. Remove the steak from the broth mixture; reserve the mixture for basting. Thread the steak cubes onto skewers, alternating with the squash, mushrooms, and bell pepper.

4. Grill the skewers about 6 inches from the heat source for 3 minutes on one side; turn and brush with the broth mixture. Grill for 3

minutes on the second side. Turn and brush with the broth mixture on the other side.

5. Grill on the other two sides for 1 to 2 minutes each, brushing with the broth mixture right after the turn, until the beef registers 145°F for medium on a meat thermometer. Discard any remaining broth mixture, and serve immediately.

COOKING TIP: For gas grills, medium heat is about 350°F. If you are cooking over charcoal, let the coals burn down for about 25 minutes, or until you can hold your hand (carefully) over the coals at the height of the rack for about 6 seconds until you are forced to pull it away. Just don't burn yourself!

Per serving: Calories 279; Fat 12g (with 39% calories from fat); Saturated fat 4g; Monounsaturated fat 3g; Carbs 19g; Sodium 79mg; Dietary fiber 3g; Protein 20g; Cholesterol 64mg; Vitamin A 39% DV; Vitamin C 149% DV; Sugar 15g

Beef and Mushroom Burger

GLUTEN-FREE, NUT-FREE

SERVES 4 / **PREP TIME:** 13 minutes / **COOK TIME:** 17 minutes

This burger is more like a chopped steak, served with a knife and fork and drizzled with delicious pan gravy. Mushrooms add a meaty, umami taste, with no fat or cholesterol and lots of fiber.

1 (8-ounce) package cremini mushrooms
1 large portobello mushroom
2 scallions, minced
4 cloves garlic, minced
1 tablespoon low-sodium yellow mustard
2 tablespoons low-sodium ketchup
⅛ teaspoon black pepper
1 egg white
¾ pound extra-lean ground beef
1 cup low-sodium beef broth
1 tablespoon low-sodium Worcestershire sauce
1 tablespoon cornstarch
Pinch salt
½ teaspoon dried marjoram leaves
1 teaspoon olive oil

1. Rinse the cremini and portobello mushrooms and dry them. Trim off the stems and finely chop the mushrooms.

2. In a large nonstick skillet, sauté the mushrooms over medium-high heat until they release liquid, the volume reduces, and the liquid evaporates, about 6 minutes. Transfer the mushrooms to a large bowl and let cool slightly while you prepare the remaining ingredients.

3. Add the scallions, garlic, mustard, ketchup, pepper, and egg white to the mushrooms and mix well. Add the beef, and mix gently but thoroughly with your hands until combined.

4. Form the mixture into four patties, put on a plate, and refrigerate while you make the sauce.

5. In a small bowl, combine the broth, Worcestershire sauce, cornstarch, salt, and marjoram leaves, and set aside.

6. Heat a nonstick skillet over medium heat and add the olive oil. Add the patties and cook for 5 minutes without turning, shaking the pan occasionally.

7. Carefully turn the patties and cook for another 4 to 5 minutes, shaking the pan occasionally, until they register 160°F on a meat thermometer.

8. Remove the burgers from the pan and set them aside on a clean plate. Cover the plate to keep them warm.

9. Add the broth mixture to the skillet and bring to a simmer over medium heat. Return the burgers to the pan and simmer for 1 minute longer. Serve immediately.

SUBSTITUTION TIP: You can omit the beef broth mixture and serve these burgers on whole-wheat buns if you'd like. Just be aware that whole-wheat buns will add 140 calories, 2 grams of fat, 25 grams of carbohydrates, 3 grams of sugar, and 270 mg of sodium to this recipe, per serving.

Per serving: Calories 204; Fat 8g (with 35% calories from fat); Saturated fat 3g; Monounsaturated fat 1g; Carbs 10g; Sodium mg; Dietary fiber 1g; Protein 23g; Cholesterol mg; Vitamin A 1% DV; Vitamin C 10% DV; Sugar 4g

Mini Lasagna Cups

GLUTEN-FREE, NUT-FREE

MAKES 6 lasagna cups (serves 3) / **PREP TIME:** 12 minutes / **COOK TIME:** 18 minutes

With this clever recipe, which uses low-fat dairy and beef, and uses corn tortillas in place of long-cooking noodles, you can get some of that flavor back in your diet, and do it in under 30 minutes.

⅓ pound 98% lean ground beef
2 scallions, minced
3 cloves garlic, minced
1¼ cups low-sodium marinara sauce
1 teaspoon dried Italian seasoning
¾ cup low-fat ricotta cheese
¼ cup grated Romano cheese
6 (4-inch) corn tortillas

1. Preheat the oven to 375°F. Spray 6 standard muffin cups with nonstick cooking spray and set aside.

2. In a medium nonstick skillet, sauté the ground beef with the scallions and garlic over medium-high heat, stirring to break up the meat, until the beef is browned, about 3 minutes. Drain if necessary.

3. Stir the marinara sauce and Italian seasoning into the beef mixture. Remove from the heat, then cut the corn tortillas into thirds.

4. Dip a piece of tortilla into the meat sauce and put it into a muffin cup. Top with 2 tablespoons meat sauce. Top with one corn tortilla piece. Top with two tablespoons ricotta cheese. Add another tortilla piece, then 2 tablespoons meat sauce. Sprinkle with the Romano cheese. Repeat, filling the remaining 5 muffin cups.

5. Bake the lasagna cups for 10 to 15 minutes or until the cups are bubbling and the cheese on top is lightly browned. Transfer the muffin tin to a cooling rack.

6. Let stand for 5 minutes, then run a knife around the edges of each muffin cup and remove the mini lasagnas.

COOKING TIP: You can easily double this recipe to make more little cups. And you can freeze these mini lasagnas too. Cover tightly with freezer wrap and freeze for up to 3 months. To serve, thaw, uncover and place in muffin cups. Bake for 15 to 20 minutes at 350°F until thoroughly heated to 165°F with the meat thermometer.

Per serving: Calories 266; Fat 10g (with 33% calories from fat); Saturated fat 4g; Monounsaturated fat 0g; Carbs 26g; Sodium 357mg; Dietary fiber 3g; Protein 18g; Cholesterol 40mg; Vitamin A 15% DV; Vitamin C 18% DV; Sugar 6g

Spinach and Kale Salad with Spicy Pork

GLUTEN-FREE, NUT-FREE

SERVES 4 / **PREP TIME:** 20 minutes / **COOK TIME:** 10 minutes

Spinach and kale are packed with fiber to help reduce blood cholesterol. They make a fine and rich salad when combined with a simple mustard dressing and some spicy sautéed pork.

1 tablespoon olive oil, divided
2 tablespoons buttermilk
2 tablespoons lime juice
2 tablespoons low-sodium yellow mustard
½ teaspoon fennel seed
1 pound plain pork tenderloin
Pinch salt
⅛ teaspoon cayenne pepper
2 teaspoons chili powder
3 cups baby spinach leaves, rinsed and dried
2 cups torn kale leaves, rinsed and dried, stem removed
1 carrot, shredded
1 red bell pepper, seeded and chopped
1 tablespoon crumbled soft goat cheese

1. In a small bowl, make the dressing: Combine 2 teaspoons of the olive oil, the buttermilk, lime juice, mustard, and fennel seed, and mix well with a whisk until combined. Set aside.

2. Slice the pork tenderloin into 1-inch pieces and put into a medium bowl. Sprinkle with the salt, cayenne pepper, and chili powder.

3. Heat the remaining 1 teaspoon olive oil in a large nonstick skillet. Add the tenderloin pieces, cut side down. Cook for 4 minutes without turning.

4. Turn the pork and cook for 2 to 3 minutes or until the pork registers 150°F on a meat thermometer. Remove from the pan to a clean plate and cover with an aluminum foil tent to keep warm.

5. In a large salad bowl, toss the spinach, kale, carrot, and bell pepper. Add the salad dressing and toss to coat. Top with the pork and goat cheese, and serve immediately.

Per serving: Calories 207; Fat 9g (with 39% calories from fat); Saturated fat 2g; Monounsaturated fat 4g; Carbs 7g; Sodium 213mg; Dietary fiber 2g; Protein 26g; Cholesterol 75mg; Vitamin A 120% DV; Vitamin C 83% DV; Sugar 3g

Chile Pork with Soba Noodles

NUT-FREE

SERVES 4 / **PREP TIME:** 15 minutes / **COOK TIME:** 15 minutes

Soba noodles are typically made of buckwheat, which, despite the name, are gluten-free. But read the label, because not *all* soba noodles are made without wheat flour. Buckwheat helps improve your blood lipid profile and lowers LDL cholesterol.

3 (4-ounce) boneless top loin pork chops
Pinch salt
2 teaspoons chili powder
⅛ teaspoon cayenne pepper
1 cup low-sodium chicken broth
1 tablespoon rice wine vinegar
1 teaspoon low-sodium soy sauce
1 tablespoon cornstarch
8 ounces soba noodles
1 teaspoon toasted sesame oil
1 carrot, grated
1 red chile pepper, seeded and minced
2 scallions, chopped
1 small zucchini, sliced

1. Bring a large pot of water to a boil.

2. Trim excess fat from the pork chops and discard. Cut the chops into 1-inch cubes, and put them in a medium bowl. Toss with the salt, chili powder, and cayenne pepper, and set aside.

3. In a small bowl, combine the chicken broth, rice wine vinegar, soy sauce, and cornstarch, and set aside.

4. Cook the soba noodles according to the package directions, about 6 minutes. Drain in a colander, rinse with cool water, and set aside.

5. In a large nonstick skillet or wok over medium-high heat, heat the sesame oil. Add the pork pieces and stir-fry 3 to 4 minutes or until the pork is almost cooked. Transfer to a clean plate.

6. Add the carrot, chile pepper, scallions, and zucchini to the skillet; stir-fry for 3 to 4 minutes or until crisp-tender.

7. Add the chicken broth mixture, the pork, and the soba noodles to the skillet, and stir-fry 2 to 3 minutes or until the sauce simmers and is thickened. Serve immediately.

DID YOU KNOW? Most brands of soy sauce are not gluten-free; many are made with wheat. A good gluten-free substitute for soy sauce is tamari, a type of soy sauce made without wheat. You can usually find it in the international section of your supermarket.

Per serving: Calories 342; Fat 5g (with 16% calories from fat); Saturated fat 2g; Monounsaturated fat 0g; Carbs 49g; Sodium 542mg; Dietary fiber 2g; Protein 26g; Cholesterol 34mg; Vitamin A 71% DV; Vitamin C 32% DV; Sugar 2g

Pork and Fennel Stir Fry

NUT-FREE

SERVES 4 / PREP TIME: 20 minutes / COOK TIME: 10 minutes

Fennel contains a good amount of fiber to help lower cholesterol and lots of vitamin C and phytonutrients to support heart health. Plus, its fresh anise taste adds a subtly sweet licorice flavor to this quick-cooking stir-fry.

1 fennel bulb
1½ cups low-sodium chicken broth
1 tablespoon rice wine vinegar
1 tablespoon honey
2 tablespoons cornstarch
1 teaspoon soy sauce
12 ounces boneless top loin pork chops
Pinch salt
⅛ teaspoon white pepper
2 teaspoons olive oil
8 ounces cremini mushrooms, sliced
3 stalks celery, sliced
2 cloves garlic, minced

1. To prepare the fennel, trim the root end and cut off the stalk. Cut the bulb in half and peel off the outer skin. Slice the fennel thinly crosswise, and set aside. Finely slice the stalks, if desired. Cut some of the fennel fronds into tiny pieces with kitchen scissors, and set aside.

2. In a small bowl, combine the chicken broth, rice wine vinegar, honey, cornstarch, and soy sauce, and whisk to combine. Set aside.

3. Trim excess fat from the pork chops, and cut into 1-inch pieces. Sprinkle with the salt and white pepper.

4. Heat the olive oil in a large nonstick skillet or wok over medium-high heat. Add the pork and stir-fry until lightly browned, about 3 minutes. Remove the pork to a clean plate.

5. Add the fennel, fennel stalks if using, mushrooms, celery, and garlic to the skillet, and stir-fry for 3 to 4 minutes or until crisp-tender.

6. Stir the broth mixture, add it to the skillet, and bring to a simmer.

7. Add the pork and stir-fry 2 to 3 minutes or until the pork is cooked to at least 150°F on a meat thermometer and the sauce is thickened. Sprinkle with the reserved fennel fronds and serve immediately.

Per serving: Calories 204; Fat 7g (with 31% calories from fat); Saturated fat 2g; Monounsaturated fat 2g; Carbs 16g; Sodium 324mg; Dietary fiber 3g; Protein 19g; Cholesterol 35mg; Vitamin A 12% DV; Vitamin C 32% DV; Sugar 6g

Lemon Basil Pork Medallions

GLUTEN-FREE, NUT-FREE

SERVES 4 / **PREP TIME:** 15 minutes / **COOK TIME:** 15 minutes

Medallions of pork are cut from the tenderloin, one of the leanest cuts. In this recipe, the pork is sliced, then pounded slightly so the meat cooks more quickly. Lemon and basil are the perfect complements.

1 pound plain pork tenderloin
½ teaspoon dried basil leaves
Pinch salt
⅛ teaspoon lemon pepper
3 tablespoons cornstarch
1 teaspoon olive oil
3 cloves garlic, minced
1 cup chicken broth
3 tablespoons fresh lemon juice
1 teaspoon fresh lemon zest
3 tablespoons chopped fresh basil

1. Slice the pork tenderloin crosswise into 1-inch slices.

2. Place the slices on a piece of plastic wrap or parchment paper. Cover with another piece of plastic wrap. Put on a cutting board.

3. Using a rolling pin or meat mallet, gently pound the slices until they are about ½-inch thick.

4. On a plate, combine the dried basil, salt, lemon pepper, and cornstarch. Add the tenderloin slices and toss to coat.

5. Heat a large nonstick skillet over medium heat and add the olive oil.

6. Add half the tenderloin slices and cook until browned, about 2 minutes (it's important to not crowd the pan). Turn the pork and

cook 1 to 2 minutes on the other side. Remove from the skillet to a clean plate. Repeat with remaining pork.

7. Add the garlic to the pan and cook, stirring constantly, for 1 minute. Add the chicken broth, lemon juice, and lemon zest, and bring to a simmer.

8. Put the pork slices back in the skillet, and simmer for 2 to 3 minutes until sauce thickens slightly and is cooked to 145°F on a meat thermometer. Stir in the fresh basil leaves, and serve.

INGREDIENT TIP: Lemon pepper is a great ingredient to use in recipes that also use lemon juice and zest. It is made from lemon zest and peppercorns that are baked together. Oils from the lemon skin infuse the pepper with an intense lemony flavor.

Per serving: Calories 170; Fat 6g (with 32% calories from fat); Saturated fat 2g; Monounsaturated fat 2g; Carbs 8g; Sodium 328mg; Dietary fiber 0g; Protein 21g; Cholesterol 50mg; Vitamin A 3% DV; Vitamin C 9% DV; Sugar 1g

Pepper Pot

GLUTEN-FREE, NUT-FREE

SERVES 4 / **PREP TIME:** 15 minutes / **COOK TIME:** 15 minutes

Pepper pot is a spicy meat stew that is popular in Guyana and the Caribbean. This recipe is a one-dish stovetop meal filled with bell peppers, potato, and lots of chiles for spice. The dish is satisfying and flavorful, with nutritious ingredients.

¾ pound boneless center cut pork chops

⅛ teaspoon cayenne pepper

1 teaspoon olive oil

1 onion, chopped

4 cloves garlic, minced

1 red bell pepper, seeded and chopped

1 yellow bell pepper, seeded and chopped

2 Yukon Gold potatoes, diced

2 jalapeño pepper, seeded and minced

1 red Thai chile pepper, minced (optional)

1 (14-ounce) can no-salt-added diced tomatoes

1 cup low-sodium chicken broth

1 teaspoon Thai garlic chili paste (optional)

1 teaspoon ground cinnamon

1. Trim excess fat off the pork chops and cut the meat into 1-inch pieces. Sprinkle with the cayenne pepper.

2. Heat the olive oil in a large nonstick skillet over medium heat. Add the pork, onion, and garlic, and sauté 3 to 4 minutes or until the pork is lightly browned.

3. Add the red bell pepper, yellow bell pepper, potato, jalapeño, Thai chile pepper (if using), tomatoes, chicken broth, chili paste (if using), and cinnamon, and bring to a simmer. Reduce the heat to

medium-low and simmer 10 to 12 minutes, or until the potato is tender and the sauce is slightly thickened. Serve immediately.

DID YOU KNOW? Pepper pot is typically served over grits, which is cooked cornmeal. To make it, combine 2 cups low-sodium chicken stock with 2 cups low-fat milk and 1 teaspoon butter, and bring to a simmer. Stir in 1 cup coarse yellow cornmeal or hominy grits. Cook and stir for 10 to 15 minutes or until the mixture thickens.

Per serving: Calories 258; Fat 6g (with 21% calories from fat); Saturated fat 1g; Monounsaturated fat 1g; Carbs 28g; Sodium 104mg; Dietary fiber 4g; Protein 23g; Cholesterol 56mg; Vitamin A 29% DV; Vitamin C 149% DV; Sugar 6g

Pork Goulash

NUT-FREE

SERVES 4 / **PREP TIME:** 15 minutes / **COOK TIME:** 15 minutes

Goulash is a combination of ground meat, tomatoes, and veggies that usually simmers for hours on the stovetop; here's a shortcut version that's still super flavorful. The tomatoes are high in lycopene, which helps inhibit LDL cholesterol production, as well as vitamins A and C.

½ pound lean ground pork

2 onions, chopped

8 ounces sliced button mushrooms

4 cloves garlic, minced

3 stalks celery, sliced

½ cup grated carrot

2 teaspoons smoked paprika

Pinch salt

⅛ teaspoon white pepper

1 (14-ounce) can no-salt-added diced tomatoes

1 (8-ounce) can no-salt-added tomato sauce

2 tablespoons tomato paste

½ cup water

1 cup whole-wheat orzo

1. In a large skillet over medium-high, sauté the pork, onions, mushrooms, garlic, celery, and carrot for 4 minutes, stirring to break up the pork, until the meat is almost cooked through.

2. Add the paprika, salt, white pepper, tomatoes, tomato sauce, tomato paste, and water, and bring to a simmer. Simmer for 1 minute.

3. Add the orzo to the skillet and stir, making sure that the pasta is covered by liquid. Simmer for 10 to 12 minutes or until the pasta is cooked al dente. Serve immediately.

INGREDIENT TIP: You can buy tomato paste in a tube, which is a much more efficient way of using this ingredient. Or, if your tomato paste comes in a can, you can divide the paste into 2-tablespoon portions, and freeze some for later use.

Per serving: Calories 299; Fat 7g (with 21% calories from fat); Saturated fat 2g; Monounsaturated fat 0g; Carbs 40g; Sodium 128mg; Dietary fiber 6g; Protein 19g; Cholesterol 42mg; Vitamin A 11% DV; Vitamin C 37% DV; Sugar 10g

Thai Soba Noodles with Spring Veggies

CHAPTER SIX

Plant-Based Dishes

Vegan Ratatouille

Vegetable Lo Mein

Thai Soba Noodles with Spring Veggies

Korean Veggie Burger

Lentil Bolognese

Lentil Pilaf

Spicy Pinto Bean Quinoa Bowl

Cauliflower with Orzo and Black Beans

Mixed Bean Salad with Hummus Dressing

Mixed Green Tofu Salad with Avocado Dressing

Tofu with Chimichurri Sauce

Roasted Tofu with Tomatoes and Peaches

Soybean and Veggie Tabbouleh

Warm Soba and Tofu Salad

Seitan Stir-Fry with Broccoli and Peas

Vegan Ratatouille

VEGAN, GLUTEN-FREE, NUT-FREE

SERVES 4 / **PREP TIME:** 10 minutes / **COOK TIME:** 20 minutes

Ratatouille is a thick, French Provençal vegetable casserole with rich layers of flavor. This quick version is made with fiber-rich eggplant, summer squash, tomatoes, and bell peppers. It's delicious off the stove, but tastes even better as leftovers the next day. And as long as you add the ingredients to the pan as you prepare them, the recipe will be done in 30 minutes!

1 tablespoon olive oil
1 onion, chopped
4 cloves garlic, minced
1 red bell pepper, seeded and chopped
1 small eggplant, diced
1 yellow summer squash, diced
2 (14-ounce) cans no-salt-added diced tomatoes
3 tablespoons no-salt-added tomato paste
Pinch salt
1 teaspoon dried Italian seasoning
1 (16-ounce) can no-salt-added cannellini beans, rinsed and drained
2 tablespoons minced fresh basil
2 tablespoons pitted and sliced black olives

1. Heat a large skillet over medium heat. Add the olive oil, onion, and garlic.

2. As you finish preparing the bell pepper, eggplant, and summer squash, add them to the skillet.

3. Stir the vegetables, then add the tomatoes, tomato paste, salt, and Italian seasoning. Stir in the beans.

4. Simmer over medium heat 10 to 15 minutes, stirring frequently, until the vegetables are tender.

5. Sprinkle with the basil and olives, and serve.

COOKING TIP: Leftover ratatouille can be served in many ways. You can use it as a filling for an omelet, or put it on top of toasted whole-grain toast for breakfast. Reheat it and serve over cooked grits or a grain such as farro or quinoa.

Per serving: Calories 261; Fat 6g (with 21% calories from fat); Saturated fat 1g; Monounsaturated fat 3g; Carbs 43g; Sodium 135mg; Dietary fiber 14g; Protein 12g; Cholesterol 1mg; Vitamin A 40% DV; Vitamin C 86% DV; Sugar 13g

Vegetable Lo Mein

VEGAN, NUT-FREE

SERVES 4 / **PREP TIME:** 15 minutes / **COOK TIME:** 15 minutes

Traditional Chinese lo mein is an egg noodle dish with meat, vegetables, and a savory sauce. In this vegan version, lots of veggies like mushrooms, green beans, broccoli, and cabbage are mixed with whole-wheat noodles, cannellini beans for added protein, and a slightly sweet-salty sauce.

½ **cup low-sodium vegetable broth**
1 tablespoon cornstarch
1 tablespoon pure maple syrup
1 teaspoon low-sodium soy sauce
1 teaspoon hoisin sauce
1 teaspoon toasted sesame oil
8-ounces whole-wheat spaghetti
2 teaspoons olive oil
8 ounces sliced cremini mushrooms
2 cups bite-sized broccoli florets
2 cloves garlic, minced
2 cups green beans, cut into 1-inch pieces
2 cups chopped red cabbage
1 (16-ounce) can no-salt-added cannellini beans, rinsed and drained

1. Heat a large pot of water to boiling.

2. Meanwhile, in a small bowl, whisk together the vegetable broth, cornstarch, maple syrup, soy sauce, hoisin sauce, and toasted sesame oil. Set aside.

3. Cook the spaghetti in the water until just al dente, about 6 minutes; drain and set aside.

4. In a large nonstick skillet or wok, heat the olive oil over medium-high heat.

5. Add the mushrooms, broccoli, garlic, green beans, and red cabbage. Stir-fry for 3 to 5 minutes or until the vegetables are crisp-tender.

6. Add the cooked spaghetti and cannellini beans to the skillet, and stir-fry for 1 minute.

7. Add the sauce and stir-fry for 1 to 2 minutes or until the sauce thickens slightly. Serve immediately.

Per serving: Calories 455; Fat 5g (with 10% calories from fat); Saturated fat 1g; Monounsaturated fat 2g; Carbs 86g; Sodium 116mg; Dietary fiber 12g; Protein 22g; Cholesterol 0mg; Vitamin A 14% DV; Vitamin C 107% DV; Sugar 8g

Thai Soba Noodles with Spring Veggies

VEGAN, NUT-FREE

SERVES 4 / **PREP TIME:** 15 minutes / **COOK TIME:** 15 minutes

Enjoy takeout-caliber noodles that feature high-fiber, heart-healthy veggies. Classic Thai ingredients such as ginger, garlic, and curry paste add intense flavor to this easy-to-assemble one-dish meal.

½ cup low-sodium vegetable broth

1 tablespoon cornstarch

1 tablespoon yellow curry paste

1 teaspoon low-sodium soy sauce

⅛ teaspoon ground ginger

9 ounces soba noodles

2 teaspoons sesame oil

3 scallions, chopped

3 cloves garlic, minced

1 cup shelled edamame (see Ingredient Tip)

1 cup baby carrots, cut in half lengthwise

2 cups snow pea pods

2 cups asparagus cut into 1-inch pieces, woody ends trimmed

2 tablespoons chopped fresh chives

1. Bring a large pot of water to a boil.

2. Meanwhile, in a small bowl, whisk together the broth, cornstarch, curry paste, soy sauce, and ginger, and set aside.

3. Cook the soba noodles according to package instructions until al dente. Drain, rinse, and set aside.

4. Heat the sesame oil in a large nonstick skillet or wok over medium-high heat.

5. Add the scallions and garlic, and stir-fry for 2 minutes.

6. Add the edamame and baby carrots, and stir-fry for 3 minutes.

7. Add the snow pea pods and asparagus, and stir-fry for 3 minutes.

8. Add the noodles and the sauce, and stir-fry for 2 to 3 minutes or until the sauce thickens.

9. Sprinkle with the chives, and serve immediately.

INGREDIENT TIP: Edamame can be purchased fresh still in the pod. The little beans are easy to remove; just squeeze the sides of the pod and they slip right out.

Per serving: Calories 379; Fat 7g (with 17% calories from fat); Saturated fat 1g; Monounsaturated fat 1g; Carbs 68g; Sodium 520mg; Dietary fiber 7g; Protein 18g; Cholesterol 0mg; Vitamin A 75% DV; Vitamin C 76% DV; Sugar 7g

Korean Veggie Burger

VEGAN, NUT-FREE

SERVES 4 / **PREP TIME:** 14 minutes / **COOK TIME:** 16 minutes

Homemade veggie burgers need a solid base so they don't crumble as they cook. These burgers are held together well by their ingredients, a delicious combination of mushrooms, kidney beans, and onion, with a kick of Korean spice. But feel free to substitute any type of mushrooms, beans, and seasonings to make this recipe your own.

3 teaspoons sesame oil, divided
1 small onion, minced
4 cloves garlic, minced
1 jalapeño pepper, seeded and minced
8 ounces sliced cremini mushrooms
1 carrot, finely shredded
1 cup no-salt-added kidney beans, rinsed, drained and mashed
1 egg white
⅓ cup whole-wheat bread crumbs
1 teaspoon low-sodium soy sauce
½ teaspoon dry mustard powder
⅛ teaspoon red pepper flakes
⅛ teaspoon ground ginger
4 100% whole-wheat buns
1 tomato, sliced
4 leaves butter lettuce

1. Heat 1 teaspoon sesame oil in a large nonstick skillet over medium heat. Add the onion, garlic, jalapeño, mushrooms, and carrot.

2. Cook and stir for 8 to 9 minutes or until the mushrooms are browned, they have released moisture, and the moisture has

evaporated.

3. Transfer the mixture to a large cutting board, and chop into small pieces.

4. Put the mushroom mixture into a large bowl and add the beans, egg white, bread crumbs, soy sauce, mustard powder, red pepper flakes, and ginger, and mix well.

5. Form the mixture into four burgers. Let stand 5 minutes.

6. Add the remaining 2 teaspoons sesame oil to the same pan and heat over medium heat. Place the burgers gently in the pan and cook for 4 minutes per side, turning once, until they are browned and register at 160°F.

7. Serve on buns with tomato and lettuce.

Per serving: Calories 276; Fat 5g (with 16% calories from fat); Saturated fat 1g; Monounsaturated fat 1g; Carbs 45g; Sodium 344mg; Dietary fiber 9g; Protein 15g; Cholesterol 0mg; Vitamin A 78% DV; Vitamin C 35% DV; Sugar 6g

Lentil Bolognese

VEGAN, GLUTEN-FREE, NUT-FREE

SERVES 4 / **PREP TIME:** 10 minutes / **COOK TIME:** 20 minutes

A rich Italian tomato sauce made with ground beef or pork, onions, and herbs, Bolognese makes a comforting meal. Here, we substitute red lentils for the meat in an equally delicious and hearty nutrient-dense rendition.

¾ cup red lentils

2 teaspoons olive oil

1 onion, chopped

1 cup sliced mushrooms

2 cloves garlic, minced

1 carrot, grated

1 teaspoon dried Italian seasoning

3 cups low-sodium vegetable broth

½ cup dry red wine (optional)

8 ounces brown rice pasta or quinoa spaghetti

1 (14-ounce) can no-salt-added diced tomatoes, drained

1 (8-ounce) can no-salt-added tomato sauce

2 tablespoons chopped fresh basil

1. Sort the lentils and rinse them, then set aside.

2. Heat the olive oil in a large skillet over medium-high heat. Add the onion, mushrooms, and garlic, and cook for 2 minutes, stirring frequently.

3. Add the carrot, Italian seasoning, lentils, vegetable broth, and red wine (if using), and bring to a simmer.

4. Reduce the heat to low and cook, partially covered and stirring often, for 18 to 20 minutes or until the lentils are soft.

5. Meanwhile, bring a large pot of water to a boil, add the pasta, and cook until al dente. Drain and set aside.

6. When the lentils are soft, add the tomatoes and the tomato sauce and simmer for 2 to 3 minutes. Serve the lentil sauce over the cooked spaghetti, topped with the fresh basil.

INGREDIENT TIP: You can find pasta made out of all kinds of interesting ingredients. Pasta can be made from brown rice, chickpeas, black beans, quinoa, corn, or a combination of rice flour and potato starch. Try several kinds to find the one you like best.

Per serving: Calories 429; Fat 4g (with 8% calories from fat); Saturated fat 1g; Monounsaturated fat 2g; Carbs 79g; Sodium 97mg; Dietary fiber 16g; Protein 18g; Cholesterol 1mg; Vitamin A 75% DV; Vitamin C 37% DV; Sugar 9g

Lentil Pilaf

VEGAN, GLUTEN-FREE, NUT-FREE

SERVES 4 / **PREP TIME:** 8 minutes / **COOK TIME:** 22 minutes

Lentils are little round legumes that cook quickly and have wonderful taste and texture. They are full of fiber, protein, and the B vitamins. They simmer with the vegetables in this easy and satisfying pilaf.

1¼ cup puy lentils (see Ingredient Tip)
1 tablespoon olive oil
1 leek, white and light green parts, rinsed and chopped
8 ounces sliced cremini mushrooms
1 bay leaf
2 carrots, sliced
1½ cups frozen corn
3½ cups low-sodium vegetable broth
2 tablespoons chopped fresh basil
1 tablespoon minced fresh chives

1. Sort through the lentils to remove any small stones (often found in beans and lentils from the harvesting process). In a colander, rinse and drain the lentils, and set aside.

2. Heat the olive oil in a large saucepan over medium heat. Add the leeks, mushrooms, bay leaf, carrots, and corn, and cook for 2 minutes, stirring frequently.

3. Stir in the lentils and the broth and bring to a simmer. Reduce the heat to low, cover the pan, and simmer for 20 minutes or until the lentils are tender.

4. Remove from the heat and discard the bay leaf. Stir in the fresh basil and chives and serve.

INGREDIENT TIP: There are several different types of lentils. You can buy green, red, or yellow lentils. Then there are puy lentils, grown in France. They are a variety of green lentil and they hold their shape very well when cooked. The other types of lentils can get mushy and lose their shape.

Per serving: Calories 348; Fat 6g (with 16% calories from fat); Saturated fat 1g; Monounsaturated fat 3g; Carbs 59g; Sodium 166mg; Dietary fiber 11g; Protein 19g; Cholesterol 0mg; Vitamin A 115% DV; Vitamin C 17% DV; Sugar 7g

Spicy Pinto Bean Quinoa Bowl

VEGAN, GLUTEN-FREE, NUT-FREE

SERVES 4 / **PREP TIME:** 10 minutes / **COOK TIME:** 20 minutes

Quinoa (pronounced "keen-wah") is an ancient seed that is unique in that it is a complete protein. This means you don't need to combine ingredients, as you do with legumes and grains, to meet your protein needs. It is also gluten-free and high in fiber and essential nutrients.

1 cup quinoa
1¾ cups low-sodium vegetable broth
Pinch salt
⅛ teaspoon white pepper
1 teaspoon olive oil
1 onion, chopped
3 cloves garlic, minced
1 jalapeño pepper, seeded and minced
1 (16-ounce) can no-salt-added pinto beans, rinsed and drained
½ cup low-sodium salsa
½ cup low-sodium tomato sauce
2 teaspoons chili powder
2 tablespoons orange juice
1 avocado, rinsed, peeled, and chopped
½ cup chopped fresh flat-leaf parsley

1. Place the quinoa in a fine-mesh strainer. Run under cool water until the water runs clear.

2. In a medium saucepan over medium heat, combine the quinoa, broth, and salt and bring to a simmer.

3. Simmer for 20 minutes or until the quinoa is soft and fluffy. Remove from the heat.

4. Meanwhile, heat the olive oil in a large nonstick skillet over medium heat. Add the onion, garlic, and jalapeño pepper, and sauté for 3 to 4 minutes.

5. Add the pinto beans, salsa, tomato sauce, and chili powder and bring to a simmer. Simmer, stirring frequently, until the vegetables are tender.

6. Stir the orange juice into the quinoa, and then spoon into bowls. Top with the bean mixture, avocado, and parsley, and serve immediately.

Per serving: Calories 446; Fat 12g (with 23% calories from fat); Saturated fat 2g; Monounsaturated fat 3g; Carbs 69g; Sodium 181mg; Dietary fiber 14g; Protein 20g; Cholesterol 0mg; Vitamin A 30% DV; Vitamin C 75% DV; Sugar 3g

Cauliflower with Orzo and Black Beans

VEGETARIAN, NUT-FREE

SERVES 4 / **PREP TIME:** 12 minutes / **COOK TIME:** 18 minutes

This heart-healthy meal is prepared all in one pan on the stovetop. Garlicky sautéed cauliflower simmers with black beans, orzo, herbs, and veggies for a dinner that is as satisfying as it is nutritious.

2 teaspoons olive oil

3 cups fresh cauliflower florets, in bite-sized pieces

3 cloves garlic, minced

1 yellow bell pepper, seeded and chopped into bite-sized pieces

1 (16-ounce) can no-salt-added black beans, rinsed and drained

3 cups low-sodium vegetable broth

1½ cups orzo

1 teaspoon dried thyme leaves

Pinch salt

⅛ teaspoon white pepper

1 (14-ounce) can no-salt-added diced tomatoes, undrained

2 cups baby spinach leaves

2 tablespoons grated Romano cheese

1. Heat the olive oil in large nonstick skillet over medium heat. Add the cauliflower and garlic and sauté about 6 minutes, stirring frequently, until the cauliflower is lightly browned. Add the bell pepper and stir.

2. Add the beans, broth, orzo, thyme, salt, and white pepper. Stir and bring to a simmer.

3. Reduce the heat to low and simmer for 8 to 10 minutes or until the orzo is cooked and the liquid is mostly absorbed.

4. Add the tomatoes; simmer for 1 minute longer.

5. Stir in the spinach; remove the pan from the heat, cover, and let stand for 1 minute.

6. Remove cover, sprinkle with the cheese, and serve immediately.

SUBSTITUTION TIP: To make this recipe vegan, just omit the cheese, or use a vegan cheese. You can also add other vegetables to this recipe, including green beans, summer squash, peas, or mushrooms.

Per serving: Calories 335; Fat 5g (with 13% calories from fat); Saturated fat 1g; Monounsaturated fat 2g; Carbs 56g; Sodium 182mg; Dietary fiber 14g; Protein 19g; Cholesterol 4mg; Vitamin A 10% DV; Vitamin C 198% DV; Sugar 6g

Mixed Bean Salad with Hummus Dressing

VEGAN, GLUTEN-FREE

SERVES 4 / **PREP TIME:** 20 minutes

An excellent source of nutrition, beans provide complete protein when combined with nuts or seeds. This fiber-rich recipe features four different kinds of beans: chickpeas, black beans, pinto beans, and edamame (otherwise known as soybeans).

½ cup no-salt-added canned chickpeas, rinsed and drained
2 cloves garlic, chopped
2 tablespoons tahini
3 tablespoons lime juice
2 tablespoons water
2 teaspoons toasted sesame oil
½ teaspoon ground cumin
1 (16-ounce) can no-salt-added black beans
1 (16-ounce) can no-salt-added pinto beans
1 cup fresh or frozen green beans, thawed and drained
1 cup frozen edamame, thawed, drained, and shelled
6 cups mixed salad greens
¼ cup unsalted sunflower seeds (optional)

1. In a blender or food processor, combine the chickpeas, garlic, tahini, lime juice, water, sesame oil, and cumin. Blend or process until smooth. You can add more water if you'd like to thin the dressing to your desired consistency.

2. Rinse and drain the beans. In a large salad bowl, toss the black beans, pinto beans, and edamame with the salad greens and drizzle with half of the dressing; toss again.

3. Sprinkle the salad with the sunflower seeds (if using) and serve with remaining dressing.

INGREDIENT NOTE: Some people with nut allergies can be sensitive to sunflower seeds. If you have any question about using this ingredient, don't.

DID YOU KNOW? If you are concerned about combining proteins on a vegan or vegetarian diet, you don't need to worry. You do not have to eat meals comprised of complete proteins at every meal. Just strive to get the full complement of amino acids every day. Eat a varied diet for the best nutrition.

Per serving: Calories 486; Fat 11g (with 20% calories from fat); Saturated fat 2g; Monounsaturated fat 1g; Carbs 74g; Sodium 97mg; Dietary fiber 23g; Protein 29g; Cholesterol 0mg; Vitamin A 119% DV; Vitamin C 47% DV; Sugar 2g

Mixed Green Tofu Salad with Avocado Dressing

VEGETARIAN, GLUTEN-FREE, NUT-FREE

SERVES 4 / **PREP TIME:** 20 minutes / **COOK TIME:** 10 minutes

A complete protein, tofu is bean curd, made from soybeans. It easily takes on the flavor of its seasonings and is often grilled or sautéed to create a pleasing texture. In this recipe, tangy, creamy avocado dressing pairs perfectly with crisp tofu and fresh greens.

1 avocado, pitted, peeled, and chopped
¼ cup buttermilk
¼ cup nonfat plain Greek yogurt
2 tablespoons rinsed and chopped fresh cilantro
2 tablespoons fresh lime juice
1 (16-ounce) package extra-firm tofu, drained
2 teaspoons olive oil
1 teaspoon paprika
¼ teaspoon garlic powder
¼ teaspoon ground mustard
3 cups rinsed and torn Lacinato kale leaves
4 cups rinsed baby spinach leaves
3 cups rinsed arugula
1 (16-ounce) can no-salt-added black beans, rinsed and drained
2 cups grape tomatoes

1. In a food processor or blender, combine the avocado, buttermilk, yogurt, cilantro, and lime juice, and process or blend until smooth. Set the dressing aside.

2. Press the tofu between several sheets of paper towels to remove more moisture. Cut the tofu into 1½-inch cubes.

3. Heat the olive oil in a large nonstick skillet over medium-high heat. Add the paprika, garlic powder, and mustard and stir. Then gently

add the tofu cubes.

4. Sauté the tofu, stirring frequently, until the cubes are crisp and brown, 8 to 10 minutes. Remove from the heat.

5. In a large salad bowl, toss the kale, spinach, arugula, black beans, and tomatoes. Add half of the dressing and toss again.

6. Top with the tofu and drizzle with the remaining dressing. Serve.

INGREDIENT TIP: Some health experts recommend that consumers avoid tofu, because it can be made from genetically modified (GMO) soybeans. The modification helps the plant withstand herbicide applications in the farm field, but its health effects on humans is not known. When you buy tofu, look for a label that says it is non-GMO.

Per serving: Calories 435; Fat 15g (with 31% calories from fat); Saturated fat 2g; Monounsaturated fat 3g; Carbs 47g; Sodium 89mg; Dietary fiber 16g; Protein 28g; Cholesterol 2mg; Vitamin A 130% DV; Vitamin C 123% DV; Sugar 5g

Tofu with Chimichurri Sauce

VEGAN, GLUTEN-FREE, NUT-FREE

SERVES 4 / **PREP TIME:** 15 minutes / **COOK TIME:** 10 minutes

Chimichurri sauce, which originated in Argentina, is a bright green sauce made from an abundance of herbs and garlic. It adds intense flavor and color to grilled tofu. The fresh herbs are full of vitamins.

½ **cup packed fresh parsley leaves**
⅓ **cup packed fresh basil leaves**
3 tablespoons fresh chopped chives
1 teaspoon fresh oregano leaves
3 scallions, chopped
2 tablespoons lime juice
1 tablespoon pure maple syrup
2 cloves garlic
2 tablespoons water
⅛ **teaspoon red pepper flakes**
Pinch salt
24 ounces extra-firm tofu, drained
1 teaspoon olive oil
1 teaspoon smoked paprika
¼ **teaspoon ground turmeric**

1. In a blender or food processor, combine the parsley, basil, chives, oregano, scallions, lime juice, maple syrup, garlic, water, red pepper flakes, and salt. Blend or process until the herbs are finely chopped. Set aside.

2. Press the tofu between sheets of paper towels to remove more moisture. Cut the tofu into 4 slices.

3. In a nonstick skillet, heat the olive oil over medium-high heat. Add the paprika and turmeric and stir.

4. Add the tofu slices. Cook for 5 minutes on one side, then turn and cook for 5 minutes on the second side. (Note: You can also grill the tofu. To do this, combine the olive oil, paprika, and turmeric, and brush it on the tofu slices before grilling over medium heat, 5 minutes on each side.)

5. Plate the tofu, drizzle with the chimichurri sauce, and serve immediately.

Per serving: Calories 194; Fat 11g (with 49% calories from fat); Saturated fat 1g; Monounsaturated fat 1g; Carbs 10g; Sodium 60mg; Dietary fiber 2g; Protein 18g; Cholesterol 0mg; Vitamin A 40% DV; Vitamin C 41% DV; Sugar 5g

Roasted Tofu with Tomatoes and Peaches

VEGAN, GLUTEN-FREE, NUT-FREE

SERVES 4 / **PREP TIME:** 10 minutes / **COOK TIME:** 20 minutes

Tofu is a perfect background to many flavors because of its blandness. Tomatoes and peaches, both high in vitamin C and fiber, are delicious accompaniments for crisp-roasted tofu.

1 (16-ounce) package extra-firm tofu, drained
1 tablespoon pure maple syrup
1 teaspoon sesame oil
1 teaspoon paprika
¼ teaspoon ground ginger
⅛ teaspoon cayenne pepper
Pinch ground cinnamon
2 cups yellow or red cherry tomatoes
1 cup grape tomatoes
3 peaches, peeled and sliced (see <u>Ingredient Tip</u>)
2 tablespoons fresh lemon juice
Pinch salt

1. Preheat the oven to 425°F. Line a baking sheet with aluminum foil and set aside.

2. Press the tofu between sheets of paper towel to remove excess moisture. Cut the tofu into 4 slices. Place on the prepared baking sheet.

3. In a small bowl, combine the maple syrup, sesame oil, paprika, ginger, cayenne pepper, and cinnamon, and mix well. Brush onto the tofu slices.

4. Surround the tofu with the tomatoes and peaches. Sprinkle the fruit with the lemon juice and salt.

5. Roast for 18 to 20 minutes, or until the tofu is lightly browned and the fruit is soft. Check that the tofu is not getting too browned in the last 5 minutes.

6. Serve the tofu topped with the fruit mixture.

SUBSTITUTION TIP: Cherry and grape tomatoes are delicious year-round, but peaches are only in season a few months of the year. During that time, you could substitute sliced fresh pears, nectarines, or plums if you can't find good ripe peaches.

Per serving: Calories 198; Fat 8g (with 36% calories from fat); Saturated fat 1g; Monounsaturated fat 5g; Carbs 23g; Sodium 15mg; Dietary fiber 4g; Protein 13g; Cholesterol 0mg; Vitamin A 32% DV; Vitamin C 40% DV; Sugar 18g

Soybean and Veggie Tabbouleh

VEGETARIAN, NUT-FEE

SERVES 4 / **PREP TIME:** 15 minutes / **COOK TIME:** 15 minutes

A Mediterranean mainstay, tabbouleh is a salad made with bulgur, which is cracked wheat, parsley and mint, and lots of healthy vegetables. This recipe also adds soybeans, which makes it a complete protein.

1 cup medium grind bulgur (see Ingredient Tip)
1¾ cups low-sodium vegetable broth
Pinch salt
1 (12-ounce) package frozen shelled edamame
1 cucumber, peeled, seeded, and diced
2 large tomatoes, chopped
1 orange bell pepper, seeded and chopped
1 yellow summer squash, chopped
4 scallions, sliced
¼ cup chopped fresh flat-leaf parsley
2 tablespoons chopped fresh mint
⅓ cup low-fat plain Greek yogurt
3 tablespoons buttermilk
3 tablespoons orange juice
2 tablespoons low-sodium yellow mustard
1 tablespoon olive oil
1 tablespoon honey

1. In a medium saucepan, combine the bulgur, broth, and salt, and bring to a simmer over medium heat. Reduce the heat to low, partially cover the pan, and cook for 15 minutes or until the bulgur is tender. When the bulgur is tender, remove from the heat, cover, and let stand while you prepare the rest of the salad.

2. Meanwhile, cook the edamame according to package directions and place in a large bowl.

3. Add the cucumber, tomatoes, bell pepper, squash, scallions, parsley, and mint to the bowl with the edamame, and toss to combine. Add the cooked bulgur.

4. In a small bowl, combine the yogurt, buttermilk, orange juice, mustard, olive oil, and honey, and mix well. Pour over the salad, toss to coat, and serve.

> **INGREDIENT TIPS:** Some bulgur is finely ground; other brands are coarsely ground and need more cooking time. Some brands tell you to soak the bulgur, others that it be cooked directly from the package. Some brands require overnight soaking, in which case you'll need to plan ahead. And to seed a cucumber, cut it in half and use a spoon to scoop out the seeds.

Per serving: Calories 389; Fat 9g (with 21% calories from fat); Saturated fat 1g; Monounsaturated fat 3g; Carbs 51g; Sodium 213mg; Dietary fiber 15g; Protein 26g; Cholesterol 1mg; Vitamin A 35% DV; Vitamin C 128% DV; Sugar 14g

Warm Soba and Tofu Salad

VEGAN, GLUTEN-FREE, NUT-FREE

SERVES 4 / **PREP TIME:** 20 minutes / **COOK TIME:** 10 minutes

This satisfying salad is delicious and easy to make. Tofu contains lots of calcium, which can help raise HDL cholesterol and lower LDL cholesterol. And the veggies not only give this dish jewel-toned hues: the added fiber keeps you feeling full longer.

8 ounces soba noodles
3 tablespoons orange juice
2 tablespoons low-sodium yellow mustard
1 tablespoon fresh lemon juice
1 tablespoon pure maple syrup
1 teaspoon dried thyme leaves
⅛ teaspoon black pepper
1 tablespoon sesame oil
8 ounces firm tofu, drained and cut into 1-inch pieces
3 cups chopped red cabbage
1 red bell pepper, seeded and chopped
1 carrot, grated
3 scallions, chopped
4 cups mixed salad greens

1. Bring a large pot of water to a boil. Add the soba noodles and cook according to package directions. Drain, rinse with warm water, drain again, and put into a serving bowl.

2. Meanwhile, in a small bowl, combine the orange juice, mustard, lemon juice, maple syrup, thyme, and black pepper, and mix well.

3. Heat a large nonstick skillet over medium heat. Add the sesame oil.

4. Add the tofu cubes and cook for 2 minutes, stirring occasionally.

5. Add the cabbage, red bell pepper, and carrot; cook and stir for 3 to 4 minutes longer. Add the orange juice mixture and bring to a simmer.

6. Place the tofu and vegetable mixture and scallions in the serving bowl with the soba noodles and toss.

7. Serve over the salad greens.

INGREDIENT TIP: Watch out for the sodium content in soba noodles; many can provide 25 percent of your daily sodium consumption in just one 2-ounce serving! Always read package labels when you buy foods, especially if you are trying something new.

Per serving: Calories 335; Fat 7g (with 19% calories from fat); Saturated fat 1g; Monounsaturated fat 2g; Carbs 60g; Sodium 356mg; Dietary fiber 3g; Protein 16g; Cholesterol 0mg; Vitamin A 217% DV; Vitamin C 140% DV; Sugar 9g

Seitan Stir-Fry with Broccoli and Peas

VEGAN, NUT-FREE

SERVES 4 / **PREP TIME:** 20 minutes / **COOK TIME:** 10 minutes

Seitan is a high-protein meat substitute made from wheat gluten. It lacks strong flavor, so it can be worked into almost any cuisine. In this healthy stir-fry, it's paired with broccoli, two kinds of peas, ginger, soy sauce, and lemongrass to create a distinct Asian-style flavor profile.

½ **cup low-sodium vegetable broth**
2 **tablespoons rice wine vinegar**
1 **tablespoon grated peeled ginger root**
1 **tablespoon cornstarch**
2 **cloves garlic, minced**
1 **teaspoon low-sodium soy sauce**
1 **tablespoon olive oil**
1 **(8-ounce) package seitan, cut into 2-inch strips**
3 **cups broccoli florets**
2 **stalks lemongrass, peeled and chopped**
2 **cups snow pea pods**
2 **cups frozen baby peas**

1. In a small bowl, combine the broth, vinegar, ginger root, cornstarch, garlic, and soy sauce, and mix well. Set aside.

2. Heat a large nonstick skillet or wok over medium heat. Add the olive oil.

3. Add the seitan to the skillet and stir-fry for 2 minutes. Then add the broccoli florets and the lemongrass. Stir-fry for 3 to 4 minutes longer.

4. Add the pea pods and frozen peas to the skillet; stir-fry for 4 to 5 minutes or until the vegetables are crisp-tender.

5. Stir the sauce and add it to the skillet. Stir-fry for 1 to 2 minutes longer or until the sauce thickens. Serve immediately.

INGREDIENT TIP: Lemongrass is actually a grass that is used as an ingredient in Asian cooking. To prepare it, trim off the top and the root end. Peel the bottom 4 inches of each stalk and chop or mince before adding to the recipes.

Per serving: Calories 346; Fat 6g (with 16% calories from fat); Saturated fat 2g; Monounsaturated fat 2g; Carbs 23g; Sodium 188mg; Dietary fiber 10g; Protein 50g; Cholesterol 0mg; Vitamin A 24% DV; Vitamin C 109% DV; Sugar 9g

Grilled Sweet Potatoes and Peppers

CHAPTER SEVEN

Potatoes, Pasta, and Grains

Smashed Baby Potatoes

Skillet-Roasted Sweet Potatoes

Mashed Sweet Potatoes with Nut and Seed Topping

Grilled Sweet Potatoes and Peppers

One-Pot Veggie Pasta

Pasta Puttanesca

Vegetable Egg Fried Rice

Green Rice Salad with Tomatoes

Farro Veggie Pilaf

Buckwheat Veggie Pilaf

Amaranth with Artichokes and Garlic

Fruited Quinoa Salad

Warm Teff Chutney Salad

Teff with Broccoli Pesto

Warm Barley Salad with Spring Veggies

Smashed Baby Potatoes

VEGETARIAN, GLUTEN-FREE, NUT-FREE

SERVES 4 / **PREP TIME:** 5 minutes / **COOK TIME:** 25 minutes

Red and yellow potatoes serve up more nutrition than white potatoes. They are high in anthocyanin and carotenoids, which are antioxidants, and potassium, which helps regulate blood pressure. This recipe makes potatoes that are meltingly tender with a crisp crust. And while this recipe uses butter, it's a small amount, so it adds minimal saturated fat while providing great flavor.

1 pound baby red and yellow potatoes, scrubbed and cut in half
1 cup low-sodium vegetable stock
2 tablespoons low-sodium yellow mustard
1 tablespoon melted butter
1 tablespoon lemon juice

1. Preheat the oven to 425°F.

2. Place the potatoes, cut side down, on a rimmed baking sheet. Pour the stock around the potatoes, and cover the cookie sheet with heavy-duty foil.

3. Roast the potatoes for 18 to 22 minutes, or until they are tender when pierced with a fork.

4. Meanwhile, in a small bowl, combine the mustard, melted butter, and lemon juice. Mix together and set aside.

5. Take the potatoes out of the oven; turn the oven to broil.

6. Remove the foil and, using a glass or a fork, gently press down on each potato to flatten it. (Don't press so hard you break the potatoes into pieces.)

7. Brush the mustard mixture onto the potatoes.

8. Broil the potatoes 6 inches from the heat source for 2 to 4 minutes, watching carefully, until they are browned and crisp. Serve immediately.

DID YOU KNOW? The most nutrients in a potato are in its skin and in the flesh directly under the skin. The skin has most of the fiber, so always scrub it and eat it when you prepare potatoes. Potatoes are a good source of vitamin B_6, vitamin C, and iron.

Per serving: Calories 122; Fat 3g (with 22% calories from fat); Saturated fat 2g; Monounsaturated fat 1g; Carbs 22g; Sodium 125mg; Dietary fiber 3g; Protein 2g; Cholesterol 8mg; Vitamin A 2% DV; Vitamin C 41% DV; Sugar 2g

Skillet-Roasted Sweet Potatoes

VEGAN, GLUTEN-FREE, NUT-FREE

SERVES 4 / **PREP TIME:** 10 minutes / **COOK TIME:** 20 minutes

Sweet potatoes are good for you because they are rich in vitamin A, which helps decrease cholesterol concentration in the liver. They have more vitamin A than white or red potatoes. Sweet potatoes are full of fiber too, and they taste delicious.

2 medium sweet potatoes
1 tablespoon fresh lemon juice
2 teaspoons olive oil
Pinch salt
⅛ teaspoon white pepper
3 tablespoons chopped fresh flat-leaf parsley

1. Scrub the sweet potatoes under cool, running water. Cut off any damaged areas. Don't peel the potatoes.

2. Cut the potatoes into bite-sized pieces, and sprinkle with the lemon juice.

3. Heat the olive oil over medium heat in a large nonstick skillet.

4. Add the potatoes, and sprinkle with the salt and white pepper.

5. Cook the potatoes, stirring often, for 15 to 20 minutes, or until they are tender when pierced with a fork and the outsides are crisp.

6. Remove from the heat, sprinkle with the parsley, and serve immediately.

Per serving: Calories 78; Fat 2g (with 23% calories from fat); Saturated fat 0g; Monounsaturated fat 2g; Carbs 14g; Sodium 37mg; Dietary fiber 2g; Protein 1g; Cholesterol 0mg; Vitamin A 189% DV; Vitamin C 12% DV; Sugar 3g

Mashed Sweet Potatoes with Nut and Seed Topping

VEGETARIAN, GLUTEN-FREE

SERVES 4 / **PREP TIME:** 10 minutes / **COOK TIME:** 20 minutes

Already sweet mashed sweet potatoes are often topped with brown sugar and marshmallows. Instead, choose delicious nuts and seeds to add a crunchy contrast along with lots of fiber to this heart-healthy ingredient.

1 (16-ounce) bag diced sweet potatoes (see Ingredient Tip)
1 teaspoon unsalted butter
2 tablespoons flaxseed
2 tablespoons chopped walnuts
1 tablespoon sesame seeds
1 tablespoon chia seeds
½ teaspoon ground cinnamon
⅛ teaspoon ground nutmeg
3 tablespoons natural unsweetened applesauce
2 tablespoons apple juice
Pinch salt

1. Rinse the sweet potatoes. Put them in a large saucepan and add water to cover. Bring to a boil over high heat; reduce heat to low, partially cover, and simmer for 10 to 15 minutes or until the potatoes are soft.

2. Meanwhile, heat the butter in a large skillet over medium heat. Add the flaxseed, walnuts, sesame seeds, and chia seeds. Sauté for 2 to 3 minutes, stirring constantly, until the mixture is fragrant. Transfer the mixture into a small bowl and set aside.

3. When they are soft, drain the potatoes, and put them in a large bowl. Add the applesauce, apple juice, and salt, and mash the potatoes until smooth. Sprinkle with the nut topping and serve.

INGREDIENT TIP: To make this recipe in 30 minutes, you should buy diced potatoes, either refrigerated or frozen; many large supermarkets carry them. If you want to peel and dice 2 large whole sweet potatoes yourself, add about 10 to 15 minutes to the preparation time.

Per serving: Calories 193; Fat 8g (with 37% calories from fat); Saturated fat 1g; Monounsaturated fat 1g; Carbs 29g; Sodium 65mg; Dietary fiber 7g; Protein 4g; Cholesterol 3mg; Vitamin A 318% DV; Vitamin C 10% DV; Sugar 7g

Grilled Sweet Potatoes and Peppers

VEGAN, GLUTEN-FREE, NUT-FREE

SERVES 4 / **PREP TIME:** 16 minutes / **COOK TIME:** 14 minutes

Grilling thin slices of sweet potatoes cuts way down on the cooking time and adds a great smoky flavor to this healthy root vegetable. Bell peppers cook alongside the sweet spuds on the grill. This recipe provides more than 500 percent of your DV of vitamin A!

2 medium-sized sweet potatoes, peeled
1 red bell pepper, seeded and cut into quarters
1 yellow bell pepper, seeded and cut into quarters
1 orange bell pepper, seeded and cut into quarters
1 tablespoon pure maple syrup
2 teaspoons olive oil
Pinch salt
¼ cup chopped fresh basil leaves

1. Prepare and preheat grill to medium.

2. Slice the sweet potatoes on a diagonal into ¼-inch slices.

3. In a large bowl, combine the sweet potato slices and the bell pepper quarters. Drizzle with the maple syrup, olive oil, and salt, and toss.

4. Place the potato slices on the grill, followed by the bell pepper quarters (skin-side down).

5. Cover the grill and cook for 4 to 5 minutes or until the vegetables have grill marks.

6. Turn the vegetables, cover the grill, and cook for 4 to 6 minutes until the vegetables have softened. The bell peppers will probably be ready before the sweet potatoes are done, so check them frequently.

7. Remove the veggies from the grill as they cook. Slice the bell peppers into strips before serving.

8. Sprinkle with the basil and serve.

Per serving: Calories 117; Fat 3g (with 23% calories from fat); Saturated fat 0g; Monounsaturated fat 2g; Carbs 22g; Sodium 52mg; Dietary fiber 4g; Protein 2g; Cholesterol 0mg; Vitamin A 243% DV; Vitamin C 193% DV; Sugar 9g

One-Pot Veggie Pasta

VEGETARIAN, NUT-FREE

SERVES 4 / **PREP TIME:** 15 minutes / **COOK TIME:** 10 minutes

Here's a perfect midweek meal. Cooking pasta right in the same pot as the other ingredients is not only easier, but makes the pasta more flavorful because it absorbs flavors from the sauce as it cooks. This colorful dish is also high in fiber.

1 tablespoon olive oil
1 onion, chopped
2 cloves garlic, minced
1 (8-ounce) package sliced mushrooms
2 yellow bell peppers, seeded and chopped
3 tomatoes, cored and chopped
1¾ cups low-sodium vegetable broth
1 teaspoon dried Italian seasoning
⅛ teaspoon black pepper or
cayenne pepper
8 ounces whole-wheat spaghetti
2 cups rinsed arugula
¼ cup grated Parmesan cheese

1. Heat a large saucepan over medium heat and add the olive oil.

2. Add the onion, garlic, and mushrooms, and cook and stir for 2 to 3 minutes.

3. Add the bell peppers and tomatoes, and cook and stir for 3 minutes.

4. Add the broth, Italian seasoning, and black pepper, and bring to a simmer.

5. Add the spaghetti, making sure the pasta is submerged in the cooking liquid. Bring to a simmer and cook for 10 to 12 minutes,

stirring occasionally, until the pasta is cooked al dente (see Substitution Tip).

6. Turn off the heat, and stir in the arugula until it is wilted.

7. Serve immediately with the Parmesan cheese sprinkled on top.

SUBSTITUTION TIP: To make this recipe gluten-free, substitute a non-wheat pasta. You can use pasta made from brown rice, lentils, quinoa, or chickpeas. The cooking time may be slightly less with these alternative pastas; check the box and cook about 2 to 3 minutes longer than the suggested time since pasta cooks more slowly when it is mixed with other ingredients.

Per serving: Calories 337; Fat 7g (with 19% calories from fat); Saturated fat 2g; Monounsaturated fat 3g; Carbs 60g; Sodium 228mg; Dietary fiber 4g; Protein 15g; Cholesterol 6mg; Vitamin A 24% DV; Vitamin C 313% DV; Sugar 6g

Pasta Puttanesca

NUT-FREE

SERVES 4 / **PREP TIME:** 15 minutes / **COOK TIME:** 10 minutes

It's not easy to make this recipe low-fat, because it uses olives and anchovy paste. However, they *are* good sources of healthy monounsaturated fat. By reducing the quantities and adding more veggies, the recipe is more balanced and remains on the lighter side —and it remains as mouthwatering.

8 ounces whole-wheat spaghetti
1 tablespoon olive oil
1 onion, chopped
3 cloves garlic, minced
2 cups grape tomatoes
2 tablespoons chopped Kalamata olives
1 tablespoon capers, rinsed and drained
1 teaspoon anchovy paste
1 (14-ounce) can no-salt-added diced tomatoes, undrained
3 tablespoons no-salt-added tomato paste
⅛ teaspoon red pepper flakes
3 tablespoons minced fresh basil leaves

1. Bring a large pot of water to a boil. Add the spaghetti and cook until al dente, about 7 minutes. Drain and set aside.

2. Meanwhile, heat the olive oil in a large nonstick skillet over medium heat.

3. Add the onion and garlic, and cook and stir for 3 minutes.

4. Add the grape tomatoes, olives, capers, anchovy paste, diced tomatoes, tomato paste, and red pepper flakes, and bring to a simmer. Simmer for 5 minutes.

5. Add the pasta and toss to combine. Sprinkle with the basil and serve.

> **SUBSTITUTION TIP:** If you dislike anchovies, you can substitute Worcestershire sauce instead. Or try using umeboshi, pickled plums from Japan that have a very salty flavor. The sodium content will increase if you use these substitutions.

Per serving: Calories 290; Fat 5g (with 16% calories from fat); Saturated fat 1g; Monounsaturated fat 3g; Carbs 56g; Sodium 167mg; Dietary fiber 3g; Protein 11g; Cholesterol 1mg; Vitamin A 21% DV; Vitamin C 41% DV; Sugar 7g

Vegetable Egg Fried Rice

VEGETARIAN, GLUTEN-FREE, NUT-FREE

SERVES 4 / **PREP TIME:** 15 minutes / **COOK TIME:** 13 minutes

Fried rice is best when it's made with cooked rice that has cooled. Since it takes 35 to 40 minutes to cook brown rice, for this recipe we are using frozen brown rice, which contains just rice and water. Lots of veggies add fiber and nutrition to this recipe, and the eggs supply ample protein to balance it out.

1 (10-ounce) package frozen cooked brown rice, thawed
¼ cup low-sodium vegetable broth
2 teaspoons low-sodium tamari
1 teaspoon hoisin sauce
2 eggs
2 teaspoons toasted sesame oil
1 onion, chopped
3 cloves garlic, minced
1 red bell pepper, seeded and chopped
2 cups frozen baby peas
2 tablespoons minced fresh chives

1. Thaw the brown rice according to package directions, and set aside.

2. In a small bowl, combine the vegetable broth, tamari, and hoisin sauce, and set aside.

3. In a small bowl, beat the eggs.

4. Heat the sesame oil in a large nonstick skillet or wok over medium-high heat. Add the eggs and scramble 2 to 3 minutes, stirring frequently. Remove the eggs from the skillet and set aside.

5. Add the onion, garlic, and bell pepper to the skillet, and stir-fry for 2 to 3 minutes or until crisp-tender.

6. Add the thawed rice and the frozen peas to the skillet, and stir-fry for 4 minutes or until the rice is hot.

7. Add the scrambled eggs and the broth and sauce mixture to the skillet, and stir-fry 2 to 3 minutes or until everything is hot. Sprinkle with the chives, and serve immediately.

DID YOU KNOW? If you make your own rice and cool it for this recipe, be aware that improperly cooled rice can harbor *Bacillus cereus* bacteria that can make you sick. The bacteria can survive the cooking process. Cool cooked rice quickly; spread it in a shallow pan. Don't store it more than three days. And make sure that leftover rice is reheated to 165°F before you serve it.

Per serving: Calories 214; Fat 6g (with 25% calories from fat); Saturated fat 1g; Monounsaturated fat 2g; Carbs 32g; Sodium 231mg; Dietary fiber 6g; Protein 9g; Cholesterol 106mg; Vitamin A 50% DV; Vitamin C 89% DV; Sugar 7g

Green Rice Salad with Tomatoes

VEGAN, GLUTEN-FREE, NUT-FREE

SERVES 4 / **PREP TIME:** 15 minutes / **COOK TIME:** 10 minutes

In this recipe, the rice appears green because it's mixed with lots of fresh herbs. This colorful salad is simple and comes together quickly, making it perfect for a summertime lunch.

2 (10-ounce) packages frozen cooked brown rice
2 tablespoons olive oil
2 tablespoons fresh lemon juice
1 tablespoon orange juice
1 tablespoon pure maple syrup
Pinch salt
½ cup chopped fresh flat-leaf parsley
¼ cup chopped fresh basil leaves
1 tablespoon fresh thyme leaves
1 (10-ounce) package frozen baby peas, thawed
1 cup sliced celery
2 cups grape tomatoes

1. Thaw the brown rice according to the package directions.

2. Meanwhile, in a large salad bowl, combine the olive oil, lemon juice, orange juice, maple syrup, salt, parsley, basil, and thyme, and mix well.

3. Add the cooked brown rice and toss to coat.

4. Stir in the peas, celery, and tomatoes and toss again. Serve or refrigerate.

Per serving: Calories 305; Fat 9g (with 27% calories from fat); Saturated fat 1g; Monounsaturated fat 6g; Carbs 50g; Sodium 133mg; Dietary fiber 7g; Protein 9g; Cholesterol 0mg; Vitamin A 62% DV; Vitamin C 69% DV; Sugar 10g

Farro Veggie Pilaf

VEGETARIAN, NUT-FREE

SERVES 4 / **PREP TIME:** 10 minutes / **COOK TIME:** 20 minutes

This savory pilaf features fresh herbs for an extra dose of flavor and color. High-fiber farro is filling and the many textures in this dish (crunchy celery, soft mushrooms, and toothsome grains) truly satisfy.

1 cup farro
3 cups low-sodium vegetable broth
2 teaspoons olive oil
1 onion, chopped
3 cloves garlic, minced
8 ounces sliced cremini mushrooms
3 stalks celery, sliced
3 tablespoons grated Parmesan cheese
⅓ cup chopped fresh flat-leaf parsley
1 tablespoon minced fresh tarragon

1. In a medium saucepan, combine the farro and vegetable broth, and bring to a boil over medium-high heat. Reduce the heat to low, partially cover the pan, and simmer for 18 to 22 minutes or until the farro is tender.

2. Meanwhile, in a large nonstick skillet, heat the olive oil. Add the onion and garlic, and cook for 3 minutes, stirring frequently.

3. Add the mushrooms and celery, and cook for 3 minutes, stirring frequently.

4. When the farro is tender, drain it if necessary, and add to the skillet. Cook and stir for 1 minute.

5. Add the Parmesan cheese, parsley, and tarragon, stir, and serve immediately.

SUBSTITUTION TIP: If you can't find fresh tarragon for this pilaf recipe, you can substitute 1 teaspoon dried tarragon leaves. As a general rule, substitute 1 teaspoon of dried herbs for 3 teaspoons of fresh herbs.

Per serving: Calories 191; Fat 5g (with 24% calories from fat); Saturated fat 1g; Monounsaturated fat 2g; Carbs 30g; Sodium 188mg; Dietary fiber 4g; Protein 7g; Cholesterol 3mg; Vitamin A 11% DV; Vitamin C 17% DV; Sugar 6g

Buckwheat Veggie Pilaf

VEGETARIAN, GLUTEN-FREE, NUT-FREE

SERVES 4 / **PREP TIME:** 10 minutes / **COOK TIME:** 20 minutes

Buckwheat is a gluten-free grain that is high in fiber. Buckwheat groats, also called kasha, are the seeds of the plant; they are nutty and easy to cook. This tasty pilaf cooks up in 20 minutes, making it a worthy addition to your weeknight recipe rotation.

2 teaspoons olive oil
1 cup buckwheat groats (kasha)
1 onion, chopped
2 cloves garlic, minced
1 cup sliced mushrooms
1 carrot, peeled and sliced
1 cup low-sodium vegetable broth
1 cup water
1 cup frozen corn
1 tomato, chopped
½ cup shredded Havarti or Swiss cheese
⅓ cup chopped fresh flat-leaf parsley

1. In a large saucepan, heat the olive oil over medium heat. Add the buckwheat, onion, garlic, mushrooms, and carrot, and cook for 3 to 4 minutes or until the vegetables are crisp-tender.

2. Add the vegetable broth, water, and corn, and bring to a simmer. Reduce heat to low, partially cover, and cook for 12 to 15 minutes or until the broth is evaporated and the buckwheat is tender.

3. Stir in the tomato, Havarti cheese, and parsley, and serve.

Per serving: Calories 333; Fat 8g (with 22% calories from fat); Saturated fat 3g; Monounsaturated fat 3g; Carbs 58g; Sodium 87mg; Dietary fiber 7g; Protein

13g; Cholesterol 12mg; Vitamin A 67% DV; Vitamin C 44% DV; Sugar 4g

Amaranth with Artichokes and Garlic

VEGETARIAN, GLUTEN-FREE, NUT-FREE

SERVES 4 / **PREP TIME:** 10 minutes / **COOK TIME:** 20 minutes

Amaranth is high in phytosterols, which can help lower cholesterol. Paired with the strong flavors of artichokes and garlic, it makes a rich side dish that is also full of heart-healthy elements.

2½ cups low-sodium vegetable broth
1 cup amaranth
2 teaspoons olive oil
1 shallot, minced
6 cloves garlic, sliced
1 red bell pepper, seeded and chopped
1 (15-ounce) can artichoke hearts, drained and chopped
½ teaspoon dried thyme leaves
¼ cup grated Parmesan cheese

1. In a large saucepan, bring the vegetable broth to a boil over high heat. Add the amaranth and stir. Cover the pot, reduce the heat to low, and simmer for 15 to 20 minutes or until the amaranth is tender.

2. Meanwhile, in a large nonstick skillet, heat the olive oil over medium-low heat.

3. Add the shallot and the garlic, and cook and stir for 2 minutes.

4. Add the bell pepper, and cook for 2 minutes. Add the chopped artichoke hearts and thyme and cook for 2 minutes.

5. When the amaranth is tender, drain well and add to the skillet. Add the Parmesan cheese and stir. Serve immediately.

INGREDIENT TIP: Canned artichokes are high in sodium, and there are no low-sodium versions. If you can find them, frozen artichokes hearts are a good substitute; they will reduce the sodium by about 100 mg per serving. Thaw them according to package instructions, drain, and chop to use in this recipe.

Per serving: Calories 301; Fat 6g (with 18% calories from fat); Saturated fat 2g; Monounsaturated fat 1g; Carbs 48g; Sodium 221mg; Dietary fiber 11g; Protein 15g; Cholesterol 5mg; Vitamin A 23% DV; Vitamin C 49% DV; Sugar 3g

Fruited Quinoa Salad

VEGETARIAN, GLUTEN-FREE, NUT-FREE

SERVES 4 / **PREP TIME:** 10 minutes / **COOK TIME:** 20 minutes

This sweet, tart, and savory preparation of quinoa may seem unorthodox. But fresh fruit pairs beautifully with this nutty-flavored grain. In addition, pectin-rich fruits and others like grapes and berries are high in resveratrol, which can help lower cholesterol.

1 cup quinoa
2 cups water
3 tablespoons fresh lemon juice
1 tablespoon pure honey
2 tablespoons buttermilk
2 tablespoons chopped fresh mint
2 cups red grapes
1 cup cherries, pitted
2 cups fresh blueberries
¼ cup crumbled goat cheese

1. Put the quinoa in a strainer and rinse well under cool running water.

2. In a medium saucepan, combine the quinoa and the water and bring to a boil over high heat. Reduce the heat to low and simmer for 15 to 18 minutes or until the liquid is absorbed. Put the quinoa in a salad bowl.

3. Meanwhile, in a small bowl, combine the lemon juice, honey, buttermilk, and mint, and mix well. Pour over the quinoa in the bowl and toss.

4. Add the grapes, cherries, and blueberries and toss to coat. Top with the goat cheese and serve.

SUBSTITUTION TIP: You can use other fruits in this pretty salad recipe. Try using sliced strawberries, whole raspberries, cubed mango or cantaloupe. Just think about your favorite types of fruit and add them.

Per serving: Calories 272; Fat 4g (with 13% calories from fat); Saturated fat 1g; Monounsaturated fat 0g; Carbs 55g; Sodium 43mg; Dietary fiber 6g; Protein 9g; Cholesterol 5mg; Vitamin A 4% DV; Vitamin C 54% DV; Sugar 23g

Warm Teff Chutney Salad

VEGETARIAN, GLUTEN-FREE, NUT-FREE

SERVES 4 / **PREP TIME:** 15 minutes / **COOK TIME:** 15 minutes

A tiny grain from Ethiopia and Eritrea, teff contains ample fiber, as well as magnesium and manganese, minerals that are important for a healthy heart. With sweet mango chutney and curry powder as main ingredients, this flavorful salad celebrates the flavors of India.

¾ cup teff
½ cup apple juice
1 cup water
Pinch salt
½ cup mango chutney
⅓ cup low-fat plain Greek yogurt
2 tablespoons fresh lemon juice
2 tablespoons apple juice
2 teaspoons curry powder
1½ cups red seedless grapes
1 cup sliced celery
2 scallions, sliced

1. In a medium saucepan, combine the teff, apple juice, water, and salt over medium-high heat. Bring to a simmer, reduce heat to low, and simmer for 10 to 15 minutes or until the teff is tender.

2. Meanwhile, to make the dressing, in a large salad bowl combine the chutney, yogurt, lemon juice, apple juice, and curry powder and mix well.

3. Add the teff to the dressing along with the grapes, celery, and scallions. Stir gently to coat, and serve.

INGREDIENT TIP: When you buy chutney, be sure to read the nutrition label. Some chutneys are very high in sodium, depending on the brand. Chutney can be made from many different fruits; mango is the most common.

Per serving: Calories 212; Fat 1g (with 4% calories from fat); Saturated fat 0g; Monounsaturated fat 0g; Carbs 46g; Sodium 91mg; Dietary fiber 5g; Protein 6g; Cholesterol 4mg; Vitamin A 8% DV; Vitamin C 67% DV; Sugar 24g

Teff with Broccoli Pesto

VEGETARIAN, GLUTEN-FREE, NUT-FREE

SERVES 4 / **PREP TIME:** 10 minutes / **COOK TIME:** 20 minutes

Pesto is very high in heart-healthy fat, as it is made with fresh basil leaves, lots of olive oil, garlic, pine nuts, and Parmesan. This nutrient-dense version adds broccoli and reduces the oil content. Tossed with some cooked teff, it makes a simple, satisfying side dish.

3½ cups low-sodium vegetable broth, divided
1 cup teff
1½ cups broccoli florets, cut into bite-sized pieces
1 cup packed fresh basil leaves
2 tablespoons olive oil
2 tablespoons fresh lemon juice
2 tablespoons grated Romano cheese
2 cloves garlic
Pinch salt
⅛ teaspoon black pepper

1. In a medium saucepan, bring 2½ cups of the vegetable broth to a boil. Add the teff and bring back to a simmer. Reduce the heat to low and simmer for 15 to 20 minutes or until the teff is tender.

2. Meanwhile, in another medium saucepan, combine the broccoli and the remaining 1 cup vegetable broth over medium heat and bring to a simmer. Simmer for 5 to 7 minutes or until the broccoli is tender. Drain, reserving 2 tablespoons of the vegetable broth.

3. To make the broccoli pesto, put the broccoli in a food processor or blender and add the basil, olive oil, lemon juice, Romano cheese, garlic, reserved vegetable broth, salt, and pepper. Process or blend until the mixture is smooth.

4. Drain the teff, if necessary, and place in a serving bowl.

5. Toss half the broccoli pesto with the teff, and drizzle the remaining broccoli mixture over all. Serve immediately.

SUBSTITUTION TIP: You can use other green vegetables and herbs in place of the broccoli in this easy pesto recipe. Try using 2 cups of baby spinach, arugula, parsley, broccoli rabe, watercress, or peas. Also, you can serve this pesto with cooked whole-wheat pasta, or any other grain, such as farro.

Per serving: Calories 286; Fat 9g (with 28% calories from fat); Saturated fat 2g; Monounsaturated fat 4g; Carbs 41g; Sodium 168mg; Dietary fiber 5g; Protein 11g; Cholesterol 4mg; Vitamin A 10% DV; Vitamin C 85% DV; Sugar 2g

Warm Barley Salad with Spring Veggies

VEGETARIAN, GLUTEN-FREE, NUT-FREE

SERVES 4 / **PREP TIME:** 10 minutes / **COOK TIME:** 20 minutes

Pearled barley is merely barley that has had the outer hull removed. This makes it slightly less fibrous than hulled barley, but allows it to cook more quickly. And it is still a good source of fiber, B vitamins, iron, and selenium. When paired with delicate vegetables, it makes a great warm salad.

1 cup quick-cooking pearled barley
2½ cups low-sodium vegetable broth
1 tablespoon olive oil
½ pound asparagus spears, cut into 1-inch pieces, tough stem removed
4 scallions, chopped
1 cup sugar snap peas
2 cups frozen baby peas, thawed
2 tablespoons fresh lemon juice
2 tablespoons low-sodium yellow mustard
2 tablespoons apple juice
2 teaspoons fresh thyme leaves

1. In a large saucepan, combine the barley and broth over medium-high heat and bring to a boil. Reduce the heat to low, partially cover, and simmer until the barley is tender, 10 to 15 minutes.

2. Meanwhile, heat the olive oil in a large nonstick skillet. Add the asparagus, scallions, and sugar snap peas. Sauté until the vegetables are crisp-tender. Add the baby peas, and cook 1 minute.

3. In a large serving bowl, combine the lemon juice, mustard, apple juice, and thyme, and mix. Add the sautéed vegetables to the bowl.

4. Drain the barley, if necessary, and add to the bowl along with the sautéed vegetables and dressing. Toss to coat, and serve warm.

INGREDIENT TIP: Barley is sold in several forms. Hulled barley has the most fiber, but it takes up to 55 minutes to cook and it can be difficult to find. Pearled barley has the husk and bran removed, and cooks in about 40 minutes. Quick-cooking pearled barley has been steamed, so it takes only about 20 minutes to cook.

Per serving: Calories 357; Fat 5g (with 13% calories from fat); Saturated fat 1g; Monounsaturated fat 2g; Carbs 69g; Sodium 103mg; Dietary fiber 14g; Protein 12g; Cholesterol 0mg; Vitamin A 23% DV; Vitamin C 52% DV; Sugar 19g

Spicy Lentil Chili

CHAPTER EIGHT

Soups and Stews

Healthy Minestrone

Quinoa Vegetable Soup

German Potato Soup

Pumpkin Soup with Crunchy Seeds

Butternut Squash and Lentil Soup

Spicy Lentil Chili

Three Bean Soup

Curried Cauliflower Stew

Gazpacho

Carrot Peach Soup

Tuscan Fish Stew

Cioppino

Salmon Veggie Chowder

Chicken Vegetable Stew

Thai Chicken Soup

Healthy Minestrone

VEGETARIAN, NUT-FREE

SERVES 4 / **PREP TIME:** 12 minutes / **COOK TIME:** 18 minutes

Minestrone is a rich soup packed with vegetables, beans, and pasta. Red bell peppers in this recipe are high in lycopene and have lots of soluble fiber, which helps reduce cholesterol. This delicious and hearty recipe is also open to interpretation—see the Substitution Tip for inspiration.

1 tablespoon olive oil
1 onion, chopped
2 cloves garlic, minced
1 red bell pepper, seeded and chopped
1 cup chopped red cabbage
1 (15-ounce can) low-sodium cannellini beans, rinsed and drained
1 (14-ounce) can no-salt-added diced tomatoes, undrained
3 cups low-sodium vegetable broth
1 teaspoon dried basil leaves
½ teaspoon dried oregano leaves
½ teaspoon dried thyme leaves
Pinch salt
⅛ teaspoon black pepper
½ cup whole-wheat elbow macaroni
2 cups baby spinach leaves
¼ cup shredded Parmesan

1. In a large saucepan, heat the olive oil over medium heat.

2. Add the onion and garlic, and cook and stir for 3 minutes. Add the red bell pepper and cabbage, and cook and stir for 2 minutes longer.

3. Add the beans, tomatoes, broth, basil, oregano, thyme, salt, and pepper. Simmer for 3 minutes.

4. Stir in the macaroni and simmer for 7 to 9 minutes more, or until the pasta is cooked al dente.

5. Stir in the spinach leaves until they wilt, about 1 minute. Serve, topped with the Parmesan cheese.

SUBSTITUTION TIP: You can use just about any vegetable in this easy soup recipe. Try adding sliced carrots, more bell peppers, green beans, peas, sliced zucchini or summer squash, or fresh tomatoes. That's what's nice about soup: you can add almost any vegetable and it will be delicious.

Per serving: Calories 290; Fat 6g (with 18% calories from fat); Saturated fat 1g; Monounsaturated fat 3g; Carbs 45g; Sodium 188mg; Dietary fiber 11g; Protein 16g; Cholesterol 5mg; Vitamin A 40% DV; Vitamin C 125% DV; Sugar 7g

Quinoa Vegetable Soup

VEGAN, GLUTEN-FREE, NUT-FREE

SERVES 4 / **PREP TIME:** 10 minutes / **COOK TIME:** 20 minutes

Quinoa helps make this vegetable soup more substantial, and it really hits the spot on a cold winter day. Leek is a great addition to any soup, but pairs especially well with quinoa, and both add fiber that can help in your effort to lower cholesterol.

2 teaspoons olive oil
1 leek, white and light-green parts, chopped and rinsed
3 cloves garlic, minced
2 carrots, sliced ½-inch thick
3 cups low-sodium vegetable broth
2 tomatoes, chopped
¾ cup quinoa, rinsed and drained
1 sprig fresh rosemary
1 sprig fresh thyme
Pinch salt
⅛ teaspoon cayenne pepper
1 cup baby spinach leaves

1. In a large saucepan, heat the olive oil over medium heat.

2. Add the leek and garlic, and cook and stir for 2 minutes.

3. Add the carrot, broth, tomatoes, quinoa, rosemary, thyme, salt, and cayenne pepper, and bring to a simmer.

4. Reduce the heat to low, partially cover the pan, and simmer for 17 to 19 minutes, or until the vegetables and quinoa are tender. Stir in the spinach.

5. Remove the rosemary and thyme sprigs, and serve.

Per serving: Calories 191; Fat 6g (with 28% calories from fat); Saturated fat 1g; Monounsaturated fat 2g; Carbs 32g; Sodium 142mg; Dietary fiber 5g; Protein 6g; Cholesterol 0mg; Vitamin A 134% DV; Vitamin C 25% DV; Sugar 6g

German Potato Soup

VEGETARIAN, GLUTEN-FREE, NUT-FREE

SERVES 4 / **PREP TIME:** 10 minutes / **COOK TIME:** 20 minutes

Potato soup can taste quite bland if it's not made with a lot of salt—or bacon. Liberally adding herbs helps solve that problem. Rich in fiber and potassium, this nutrient-dense soup is also comforting.

2 teaspoons olive oil

2 onions, chopped

4 cloves garlic, minced

2 large Yukon Gold potatoes, rinsed and chopped

2 cups low-sodium vegetable broth

1 tablespoon low-sodium yellow mustard

1 teaspoon tamari sauce

1 tablespoon chopped fresh rosemary leaves

½ teaspoon dried sage leaves

¼ cup plain low-fat Greek yogurt

¼ cup grated extra sharp cheddar cheese

⅓ cup chopped fresh flat-leaf parsley

¼ cup vegan bacon bits (optional)

1. In a large saucepan, heat the olive oil over medium heat.

2. Add the onions and garlic, and cook and stir for 3 minutes.

3. Add the potatoes, vegetable broth, mustard, tamari, rosemary, and sage, and bring to a simmer. Simmer for 14 to 17 minutes or until the potatoes are tender.

4. At this point, some of the soup needs to be puréed, and there are many methods you can choose from. You can do this with an immersion blender, leaving some of the potato chunks whole if you'd like. You can use a potato masher right in the pot. Or put half

of the soup into a blender, cover the blender with the lid and a towel, and blend until smooth. Then pour the blended mixture back into the soup. After you have puréed the soup, stir in the yogurt and cheddar cheese.

5. Simmer the soup for 1 minute, then ladle into bowls. Garnish with the parsley and vegan bacon bits, if using.

INGREDIENT TIP: There are many different vegetarian and vegan bacon substitutes. They are made from seitan, tempeh, tofu, and other types of alternative protein. Browse the aisles of your grocery store, or look online to find some good choices. Select the one that is lowest in sodium.

Per serving: Calories 223; Fat 5g (with 20% calories from fat); Saturated fat 2g; Monounsaturated fat 2g; Carbs 37g; Sodium 208mg; Dietary fiber 6g; Protein 8g; Cholesterol 8mg; Vitamin A 7% DV; Vitamin C 31% DV; Sugar 5g

Pumpkin Soup with Crunchy Seeds

GLUTEN-FREE, NUT-FREE

SERVES 4 / **PREP TIME:** 15 minutes / **COOK TIME:** 15 minutes

Pumpkin makes a wonderful soup, but preparing it from scratch takes a lot of time and effort. Using canned pumpkin provides the perfect shortcut, so you can get this on the table at a reasonable time on a busy weeknight. The pumpkin seed topping is high in heart-healthy fat, and also delivers additional protein and calcium.

2 teaspoons olive oil, divided
1 onion, chopped
1 tablespoon fresh peeled grated ginger root
1 (15-ounce) can pumpkin (see Ingredient Tip)
2 cups low-sodium chicken stock
1 cup unsweetened apple juice
⅓ cup natural unsweetened applesauce
Pinch salt
3 tablespoons raw shelled pumpkin seeds
2 teaspoons brown sugar
⅛ teaspoon cayenne pepper

1. Heat 1 teaspoon of the olive oil in a large saucepan over medium heat.

2. Add the onion and ginger root, and cook and stir for 2 minutes.

3. Turn up the heat to medium-high and add the pumpkin, chicken stock, apple juice, applesauce, and salt. Stir and bring to a boil.

4. Reduce the heat to low and simmer for 10 to 12 minutes, stirring occasionally.

5. Meanwhile, in a small saucepan, combine the remaining 1 teaspoon olive oil, the pumpkin seeds, brown sugar, and cayenne pepper.

Heat over medium heat, stirring frequently, until the seeds are caramelized. Transfer them to a small bowl.

6. Serve the soup topped with the pumpkin seeds.

INGREDIENT TIP: Do not buy pumpkin pie filling for this recipe; it is full of sugar and emulsifiers. Oddly enough, canned pumpkin is not always made of pumpkin; it can legally be made from several kinds of squash. Some brands are made of just pure pumpkin; that's what you want for this recipe!

Per serving: Calories 149; Fat 6g (with 36% calories from fat); Saturated fat 1g; Monounsaturated fat 3g; Carbs 24g; Sodium 84mg; Dietary fiber 4g; Protein 4g; Cholesterol 0mg; Vitamin A 413% DV; Vitamin C 40% DV; Sugar 14g

Butternut Squash and Lentil Soup

VEGETARIAN, GLUTEN-FREE, NUT-FREE

SERVES 4 / **PREP TIME:** 10 minutes / **COOK TIME:** 20 minutes

Red lentils are a good choice for this soup because they are the same color as the squash, and they virtually melt into the soup. One serving of lentils per day helps naturally reduce LDL cholesterol.

1 tablespoon olive oil
1 onion, chopped
1 tablespoon peeled grated fresh ginger root
1 (12-ounce) package peeled and diced butternut squash
1 cup red lentils, rinsed and sorted
5 cups low-sodium vegetable broth
1 cup unsweetened apple juice
Pinch salt
⅛ teaspoon black pepper
¼ teaspoon curry powder
1 sprig fresh thyme
3 tablespoons crumbled blue cheese

1. In a large saucepan, heat the olive oil over medium heat. Add the onion, and cook and stir for 3 minutes. Add the ginger, squash, and lentils, and cook and stir for 1 minute.

2. Turn up the heat to medium-high, and add the broth, apple juice, salt, pepper, curry powder, and thyme. Bring the mixture to a boil.

3. Reduce the heat to low and partially cover the pan. Simmer for 15 to 18 minutes or until the squash and lentils are tender. Remove the thyme sprig; the leaves will have fallen off.

4. Purée the soup, either in a food processor, with an immersion blender, or with a potato masher. Heat again, then ladle into bowls,

sprinkle with the blue cheese, and serve warm.

Per serving: Calories 317; Fat 7g (with 20% calories from fat); Saturated fat 2g; Monounsaturated fat 3g; Carbs 52g; Sodium 280mg; Dietary fiber 9g; Protein 15g; Cholesterol 5mg; Vitamin A 180% DV; Vitamin C 74% DV; Sugar 12g

Spicy Lentil Chili

VEGAN, GLUTEN-FREE, NUT-FREE

SERVES 4 / **PREP TIME:** 10 minutes / **COOK TIME:** 20 minutes

Lentils, with their high fiber content and nutty taste, are the perfect addition to a vegan chili. You can make this recipe as fiery hot as you'd like: just add more jalapeños and red pepper flakes.

1 tablespoon olive oil
1 onion, chopped
5 cloves garlic, minced
1 jalapeño pepper, seeded and minced
1 cup red lentils, sorted and rinsed
1 tablespoon chili powder
1 teaspoon smoked paprika
⅛ teaspoon red pepper flakes
1 (14-ounce) can no-salt-added diced tomatoes, undrained
3 tablespoons no-salt-added tomato paste
1 (16-ounce) can low-sodium kidney beans, rinsed and drained
⅓ cup chopped fresh cilantro leaves

1. In a large saucepan, heat the olive oil over medium heat.

2. Add the onion, garlic, and jalapeño pepper, and cook and stir for 2 minutes.

3. Add the lentils, chili powder, paprika, red pepper flakes, tomatoes, tomato paste, and kidney beans, and bring to a boil.

4. Lower the heat, partially cover the pan, and simmer for 15 to 18 minutes, or until the chili powder has blended in and the lentils are tender. Top with the fresh cilantro and serve.

Per serving: Calories 364; Fat 5g (with 12% calories from fat); Saturated fat 1g; Monounsaturated fat 2g; Carbs 59g; Sodium 130mg; Dietary fiber 26g; Protein

22g; Cholesterol 0mg; Vitamin A 31% DV; Vitamin C 21% DV; Sugar 8g

Three Bean Soup

VEGAN, GLUTEN-FREE, NUT-FREE

SERVES 4 / **PREP TIME:** 10 minutes / **COOK TIME:** 20 minutes

Bean soups don't always have to be made only with legumes; this recipe adds leek, carrot, and tomato. Edamame and green beans are the second and third beans in this hearty soup. Edamame is rich in fiber and antioxidants, and can also help lower LDL cholesterol.

1 tablespoon olive oil
1 leek, white and light-green parts, chopped and rinsed
1 carrot, thinly sliced
1 (16-ounce) can low-sodium black beans, rinsed and drained
2 cups green beans, cut into 1-inch pieces
1 cup frozen shelled edamame
3 cups low-sodium vegetable broth
1 (14-ounce) can no-salt-added diced tomatoes
1 teaspoon dried basil leaves
1 teaspoon dried oregano leaves
Pinch salt
⅛ teaspoon black pepper

1. In a large saucepan or stockpot, heat the olive oil over medium heat.

2. Add the leek, and cook and stir for 4 minutes. Add the carrot, and cook and stir for 1 minute.

3. Add the black beans, green beans, edamame, vegetable broth, tomatoes, basil, oregano, salt, and pepper, stir to combine, and bring to a boil.

4. Reduce the heat to low, partially cover the pan, and simmer for 15 minutes or until the vegetables are tender. Serve.

SUBSTITUTION TIP: You can substitute any type of low-sodium canned beans for the black beans in this recipe. Try pinto beans, navy beans, cannellini beans, kidney beans, or garbanzo beans (chickpeas). Just drain the canned beans, rinse them, and drain again.

Per serving: Calories 245; Fat 6g (with 22% calories from fat); Saturated fat 1g; Monounsaturated fat 2g; Carbs 35g; Sodium 260mg; Dietary fiber 13g; Protein 16g; Cholesterol 0mg; Vitamin A 78% DV; Vitamin C 34% DV; Sugar 8g

Curried Cauliflower Stew

VEGAN, GLUTEN-FREE, NUT-FREE

SERVES 4 / **PREP TIME:** 15 minutes / **COOK TIME:** 15 minutes

A nutritious vegetable related to cabbage and broccoli, cauliflower is very high in fiber and plant sterols, which can help lower cholesterol in the blood. Its mildly nutty flavor blends well with almost any cuisine.

1 tablespoon olive oil
2 shallots, minced
1 tablespoon curry powder
2 cloves garlic, minced
2 carrots, sliced
1 head cauliflower, cut into florets and chopped
⅛ teaspoon white pepper
3 cups low-sodium vegetable broth
1 (14-ounce) can no-salt-added diced tomatoes, undrained
1 (15-ounce) can no-salt-added cannellini beans, rinsed and drained
½ cup chopped fresh flat-leaf parsley

1. Heat the olive oil in a large saucepan over medium heat. Add the shallots, curry powder, and garlic, and cook and stir for 1 minute.

2. Add the carrots, cauliflower florets, white pepper, vegetable broth, tomatoes, and beans, and bring to a boil over medium heat.

3. Reduce the heat, partially cover the pot, and simmer for 13 to 14 minutes or until the cauliflower is tender.

4. Using a potato masher, mash some of the soup in the pot so it thickens. Top with the fresh parsley and serve.

Per serving: Calories 247; Fat 5g (with 18% calories from fat); Saturated fat 1g; Monounsaturated fat 3g; Carbs 42g; Sodium 182mg; Dietary fiber 13g; Protein

13g; Cholesterol 0mg; Vitamin A 118% DV; Vitamin C 144% DV; Sugar 8g

Gazpacho

SERVES 4 / **PREP TIME:** 20 minutes

Gazpacho is full of nutrients, such as lycopene from the tomatoes and sterols from cucumbers, which both help reduce LDL cholesterol. This cold soup is so refreshing on a hot summer day.

4 large beefsteak tomatoes, chopped
1 cup yellow or red cherry tomatoes, chopped
1 cup grape tomatoes, chopped
1 cucumber, peeled, seeded, and chopped
3 scallions, sliced
1 clove garlic, minced
1 cup low-sodium tomato juice
1 tablespoon fresh lemon juice
1 tablespoon olive oil
Pinch salt
⅛ teaspoon white pepper
Dash Tabasco sauce
2 tablespoons chopped fresh dill

1. In a large bowl, combine the beefsteak tomatoes, cherry tomatoes, grape tomatoes, cucumber, scallions, garlic, tomato juice, lemon juice, olive oil, salt, white pepper, Tabasco, and fresh dill.

2. Use an immersion blender to blend about half of the soup. You can also mash some of the ingredients with a potato masher. Or put about ⅓ of the soup mixture into a blender or food processor. Blend or process until smooth, then return the blended mixture to the rest of the soup.

3. Serve immediately, or cover and chill for a few hours.

DID YOU KNOW? Your body will absorb more fat-soluble nutrients such as vitamin A and vitamin D if you eat a little bit of fat along with the nutrient-dense food. That's why a little bit of olive oil is added to this gazpacho recipe.

Per serving: Calories 115; Fat 4g (with 31% calories from fat); Saturated fat 1g; Monounsaturated fat 2g; Carbs 19g; Sodium 225mg; Dietary fiber 5g; Protein 4g; Cholesterol 0mg; Vitamin A 65% DV; Vitamin C 137% DV; Sugar 12g

Carrot Peach Soup

VEGETARIAN, GLUTEN-FREE, NUT-FREE

SERVES 4 / **PREP TIME:** 15 minutes / **COOK TIME:** 15 minutes

This beautifully vibrant-colored soup is teeming with vitamins A and C. Peaches also contain niacin, which can help lower LDL cholesterol and triglycerides. Serve the sweet soup warm or chilled—it's a versatile dish.

2 large carrots, peeled and chopped
2 peaches, peeled and chopped (see Ingredient Tip)
2 cups water
½ cup orange juice
2 tablespoons honey
1 sprig fresh thyme leaves
Pinch salt
⅓ cup plain low-fat Greek yogurt

1. In a large saucepan, combine the carrots, peaches, water, orange juice, honey, thyme, and salt, and bring to a simmer over medium heat.

2. Simmer the mixture for 7 to 9 minutes or until the carrots are tender.

3. Add the yogurt to the soup and remove the thyme sprig. Purée the soup, either with an immersion blender directly in the pot, or pour the soup in two batches into a blender or food processor, and holding a towel over the lid, carefully blend until smooth. Serve immediately or cover and chill for 2 hours.

INGREDIENT TIP: The easiest way to peel a peach is to cut an X into the end and drop the fruit into simmering water. Let it stay in the water for about 20 seconds, then remove it and place it into cold water. The skin will peel right off.

Per serving: Calories 102; Fat 0g (with 0% calories from fat); Saturated fat 0g; Monounsaturated fat 0g; Carbs 23g; Sodium 77mg; Dietary fiber 2g; Protein 3g; Cholesterol 0mg; Vitamin A 130% DV; Vitamin C 41% DV; Sugar 21g

Tuscan Fish Stew

PESCATARIAN, GLUTEN-FREE, NUT-FREE

SERVES 4 / **PREP TIME:** 10 minutes / **COOK TIME:** 20 minutes

Foods from the Italian region of Tuscany often feature fish, olive oil, tomatoes, basil, and artichokes. These healthy ingredients all make an appearance in this flavorful stew, which is high in protein and thickened with homemade whole-wheat bread crumbs.

1 tablespoon olive oil
1 onion, chopped
2 cloves garlic, minced
3 large tomatoes, chopped
1 bulb fennel, peeled, chopped, and rinsed
1 (14-ounce) can artichoke hearts, drained
1 bay leaf
⅛ teaspoon red pepper flakes
2 cups low-sodium vegetable broth
¾ pound halibut fillets, cubed
¼ pound sea scallops
1 slice low-sodium whole-wheat bread, crumbled
2 tablespoons chopped fresh basil
2 teaspoons chopped fresh oregano
2 tablespoons chopped fresh flat-leaf parsley

1. In a stockpot or large saucepan, heat the olive oil over medium heat.

2. Add the onion and garlic, and cook while stirring for 3 minutes.

3. Add the tomatoes, fennel, artichoke hearts, bay leaf, red pepper flakes, and vegetable broth, and bring to a simmer. Simmer for 5 minutes.

4. Add the halibut fillets, and simmer for 4 minutes. Then add the scallops, and simmer for 3 minutes, or until the fillets flake when tested with a fork and the scallops are opaque.

5. Stir in the bread crumbs, then cover the pan and remove from the heat. Let stand 3 minutes.

6. Remove and discard the bay leaf. Top the soup with the fresh basil, oregano, and parsley, and serve.

SUBSTITUTION TIP: You can substitute other types of white fish fillets for the halibut in this recipe. Try using cod, red snapper, or turbot.

Per serving: Calories 210; Fat 6g (with 26% calories from fat); Saturated fat 1g; Monounsaturated fat 2g; Carbs 28g; Sodium 247mg; Dietary fiber 10g; Protein 29g; Cholesterol 9mg; Vitamin A 24% DV; Vitamin C 43% DV; Sugar 6g

Cioppino

PESCATARIAN, GLUTEN-FREE, NUT-FREE

SERVES 4 / **PREP TIME:** 10 minutes / **COOK TIME:** 20 minutes

Cioppino is a fish stew that is full of vegetables, such as tomatoes and fennel. It usually contains a lot of shrimp, but we've added white fish fillets and even more veggies for a healthier twist on this Italian classic.

2 teaspoons olive oil

1 leek, white and light-green parts, chopped and rinsed

3 cloves garlic, minced

3 stalks celery, sliced ½ inch thick

1 bay leaf

½ teaspoon dried oregano leaves

⅛ teaspoon cayenne pepper

3 cups low-sodium vegetable broth

¼ cup white wine (optional)

1 (14-ounce) can no-salt-added diced tomatoes, undrained

½ pound red snapper fillets, cubed

¼ pound medium shrimp, peeled and deveined

¼ cup bay scallops

¼ pound mussels, cleaned

2 tablespoons fresh lemon juice

½ cup chopped fresh flat-leaf parsley

1. Heat the olive oil in a soup pot over medium heat.

2. Add the leek and garlic, and cook and stir for 3 minutes. Add the celery and cook for 1 minute longer.

3. Add the bay leaf, oregano, cayenne pepper, vegetable broth, wine (if using), and tomatoes. Bring to a simmer, and simmer for 5

minutes.

4. Add the red snapper, and simmer for 3 minutes. Add the shrimp, and simmer for 2 minutes longer. Then add the scallops and mussels. Simmer for 2 minutes longer, or until the mussels open and the shrimp curl and turn pink.

5. Remove and discard the bay leaf. Add the lemon juice, and sprinkle with the parsley. Serve hot.

INGREDIENT TIP: Most mussels sold in fish shops and in large grocery stores have been cleaned, so you no longer have to remove the beard, which is comprised of small fibers the shellfish uses to hold onto rocks. Just rinse them well.

Per serving: Calories 220; Fat 5g (with 20% calories from fat); Saturated fat 1g; Monounsaturated fat 3g; Carbs 13g; Sodium 278mg; Dietary fiber 2g; Protein 30g; Cholesterol 95mg; Vitamin A 24% DV; Vitamin C 52% DV; Sugar 5g

Salmon Veggie Chowder

PESCATARIAN, GLUTEN-FREE, NUT-FREE

SERVES 4 / **PREP TIME:** 15 minutes / **COOK TIME:** 15 minutes

This warming salmon chowder ticks all the boxes for your go-to meal on a cold fall or winter day. Its rich flavor and creamy consistency almost makes you forget that it's heart-healthy and loaded with vitamin A!

2 teaspoons olive oil
1 onion, chopped
2 cloves garlic, minced
1 carrot, sliced
1 sweet potato, peeled and chopped
3 cups low-sodium fish broth or vegetable broth
1 teaspoon dried marjoram leaves
Pinch salt
⅛ teaspoon black pepper
2 (6-ounce) skinless salmon fillets
1 cup frozen corn, thawed
1 cup low-fat milk
2 tablespoons cornstarch

1. In a large saucepan, heat the olive oil over medium heat. Add the onion and garlic, and cook and stir for 3 minutes.

2. Add the carrot, sweet potato, broth, marjoram, salt, and pepper, and bring to a simmer.

3. Simmer for 7 to 8 minutes, or until the vegetables are soft.

4. Add the salmon fillets to the soup, and simmer for 3 to 4 minutes, or until the salmon flakes when tested with a fork.

5. Remove the salmon from the pot and flake into large pieces. Return to the pot along with the corn and simmer for 1 minute.

6. In a small bowl combine the milk and cornstarch. Whisk until blended. Add to the soup and simmer for 1 minute or until the soup is thickened. Serve.

SUBSTITUTION TIP: You can substitute other types of fish for the salmon in this creamy chowder recipe. Try using red snapper, cod, or halibut fillets. The cooking time will be about the same. Always cook fish until it flakes when you insert a fork.

Per serving: Calories 333; Fat 13g (with 35% calories from fat); Saturated fat 3g; Monounsaturated fat 2g; Carbs 29g; Sodium 213mg; Dietary fiber 4g; Protein 26g; Cholesterol 52mg; Vitamin A 346% DV; Vitamin C 14% DV; Sugar 10g

Chicken Vegetable Stew

GLUTEN-FREE, NUT-FREE

SERVES 4 / **PREP TIME:** 10 minutes / **COOK TIME:** 20 minutes

In this recipe, chicken thighs are used to lend a richer, meatier taste to the stew. Feel free to roughly chop your vegetables—stews have a chunkier consistency than soups!

2 teaspoons olive oil
3 (4-ounce) boneless, skinless chicken thighs, cubed
Pinch salt
⅛ teaspoon black pepper
1 onion, chopped
2 cloves garlic, minced
2 carrots, chopped
1 sweet potato, rinsed and chopped
2 cups low-sodium chicken stock
1 cup water
1 cup frozen corn
1 cup frozen shelled edamame
1 teaspoon dried Italian seasoning
1 cup stemless torn kale leaves or baby spinach leaves
1 tablespoon fresh lemon juice

1. Heat the olive oil in a large saucepan over medium heat.

2. Sprinkle the chicken with salt and pepper, and add to the saucepan. Cook the chicken, stirring frequently, until it is browned, about 4 to 5 minutes.

3. Remove the chicken from the pan and set aside.

4. Add the onion and garlic to the pan, and cook for 2 minutes, stirring frequently. Add the carrots, sweet potato, chicken stock, water,

corn, edamame, and Italian seasoning, and bring to a simmer.

5. Return the chicken to the pan; simmer for 10 to 13 minutes, or until the vegetables are tender and the chicken is cooked to 165°F when tested with a meat thermometer.

6. Add the kale and cook for 1 minute longer. Stir in the lemon juice, and serve.

Per serving: Calories 256; Fat 10g (with 35% calories from fat); Saturated fat 2g; Monounsaturated fat 4g; Carbs 15g; Sodium mg; Dietary fiber 5g; Protein 28g; Cholesterol 72mg; Vitamin A 354% DV; Vitamin C 28% DV; Sugar 3g

Thai Chicken Soup

GLUTEN-FREE, NUT-FREE

SERVES 4 / **PREP TIME:** 10 minutes / **COOK TIME:** 20 minutes

This spicy soup uses some unusual ingredients such as lemongrass and Thai chili paste, but doesn't use high-fat coconut milk. It's satisfying and spicy and perfect for a cool night.

2 teaspoons olive oil
2 (6-ounce) boneless, skinless chicken breasts
Pinch salt
⅛ teaspoon cayenne pepper
1 lemongrass stalk, peeled and chopped
4 cloves garlic, minced
1 jalapeño chile, seeded and minced
1 red bell pepper, seeded and chopped
2 cups low-sodium chicken stock
1 cup water
2 tablespoons fresh lime juice
1 teaspoon Thai chili paste
⅛ teaspoon ground ginger

1. In a large saucepan, heat the olive oil over medium heat.

2. Sprinkle the chicken with the salt and cayenne pepper, and add it to the saucepan. Cook, turning once, until the chicken is browned, about 3 to 4 minutes per side. Transfer the chicken to a plate and set aside.

3. Add the lemongrass, garlic, jalapeño, and bell pepper to the saucepan, and cook for 3 minutes, stirring frequently.

4. Add the chicken stock and water to the saucepan, and stir and bring to a simmer. Return the chicken to the saucepan. Simmer for

10 to 12 minutes, or until the chicken is cooked to 165°F when tested with a meat thermometer.

5. Remove the chicken to a clean plate and shred, using two forks. Return the chicken to the soup.

6. Add the lime juice, chili paste, and ginger, and simmer for 2 minutes longer. Serve hot.

Per serving: Calories 134; Fat 5g (with 34% calories from fat); Saturated fat 1g; Monounsaturated fat 2g; Carbs 4g; Sodium 237mg; Dietary fiber 1g; Protein 20g; Cholesterol 49mg; Vitamin A % DV; Vitamin C % DV; Sugar 2g

Almond Strawberry Parfaits

CHAPTER NINE

Desserts

Mango Blood Orange Sorbet

Peach Melba Frozen Yogurt Parfaits

Almond Strawberry Parfaits

Curried Fruit Compote

Skillet Apple Crisp with Mixed Nuts

Salted Caramel Pear and Blueberry Crisp

Chocolate Banana Caramel Pudding

Dark Chocolate Meringues

Dark Chocolate Brownie Bites

Double Chocolate Cinnamon Nice Cream

Mango Blood Orange Sorbet

VEGAN, GLUTEN-FREE, NUT-FREE

SERVES 4 / **PREP TIME:** 5 minutes

Sorbets can be made very quickly; in fact, if you start with frozen fruit, the method is just like making a smoothie. This colorful sorbet is chock-full of vitamin C, which helps reduce total serum cholesterol, especially LDL cholesterol.

2 cups frozen mango cubes
2 tablespoons lemon juice
⅓ cup blood orange juice (see Ingredient Tip)
3 tablespoons sugar

1. In a high-speed blender or food processor, combine the mango, lemon juice, blood orange juice, and sugar, and process until smooth.

2. Serve immediately, or freeze for a denser texture.

INGREDIENT TIP: You can find blood orange juice or blood orange purée in some specialty markets, but the best way to get it is to squeeze blood oranges yourself. These oranges are quite sweet and have very red flesh and juice. You can substitute regular orange juice if you can't find blood oranges.

Per serving: Calories 100; Fat 0g (with 0% calories from fat); Saturated fat 0g; Monounsaturated fat 0g; Carbs 26g; Sodium 2mg; Dietary fiber 2g; Protein 1g; Cholesterol 0mg; Vitamin A 13% DV; Vitamin C 61% DV; Sugar 23g

Peach Melba Frozen Yogurt Parfaits

VEGETARIAN, GLUTEN-FREE

SERVES 4 / **PREP TIME:** 15 minutes / **COOK TIME:** 5 minutes

Created in the late 1800s by the legendary French chef Auguste Escoffier, in honor of the singer Nellie Melba, Peach Melba is a combination of vanilla ice cream, peaches, and raspberries. This simple parfait is full of color, flavor, and vitamin C, and in this version, the high-fat ice cream is replaced with low-fat vanilla frozen yogurt. You can make it ahead of time—or serve it immediately.

2 tablespoons slivered almonds
1 tablespoon brown sugar
2 peaches, peeled and chopped (see Ingredient Tip)
1 cup fresh raspberries
2 cups no-sugar-added vanilla frozen yogurt
2 tablespoons peach jam
2 tablespoons raspberry jam or preserves

1. In a small nonstick skillet over medium heat, combine the almonds and brown sugar.

2. Cook, stirring frequently, until the sugar melts and coats the almonds, about 3 to 4 minutes. Remove from the heat and put the almonds on a plate to cool.

3. To make the parfaits: In four parfait or wine glasses, layer each with the peaches, raspberries, frozen yogurt, peach jam, and raspberry jam. Top each glass with the caramelized almonds.

SUBSTITUTION TIP: You can substitute frozen peach slices, thawed, or canned peach slices, drained, for the fresh peaches when they are out of season. Make sure you look for frozen or canned peaches with no sugar added. You can also use frozen raspberries but be sure to buy unsweetened whole fruit.

Per serving: Calories 263; Fat 5g (with 17% calories from fat); Saturated fat 1g; Monounsaturated fat 2g; Carbs 51g; Sodium 91mg; Dietary fiber 4g; Protein 7g; Cholesterol 10mg; Vitamin A 7% DV; Vitamin C 26% DV; Sugar 24g

Almond Strawberry Parfaits

VEGETARIAN, GLUTEN-FREE

SERVES 4 / **PREP TIME:** 15 minutes / **COOK TIME:** 5 minutes

A great make-ahead dessert, this creamy parfait treat is loaded with fiber and vitamin C, even though it's sweet. Low-fat ricotta and delightfully creamy Greek yogurt add vitamin D, which can help increase HDL cholesterol levels.

¼ **cup sliced almonds**
½ **cup low-fat ricotta cheese**
½ **cup plain nonfat Greek yogurt**
3 tablespoons powdered sugar
½ **teaspoon vanilla**
Pinch salt
2 cups sliced strawberries
2 tablespoons strawberry jam
1 tablespoon balsamic vinegar

1. In a small saucepan on the stovetop or in a glass bowl in the toaster oven, toast the almonds over low heat until they are golden. Transfer to a plate and set aside.

2. In a small bowl, combine the ricotta, yogurt, powdered sugar, vanilla, and salt.

3. In a medium bowl, combine the sliced strawberries, jam, and balsamic vinegar, and mix gently.

4. Make the parfaits by layering the ricotta mixture and the strawberry mixture into 4 parfait or wine glasses. Top each glass with the toasted almonds, and serve. You can make this recipe ahead of time and chill it up to 3 hours.

Per serving: Calories 158; Fat 6g (with 34% calories from fat); Saturated fat 2g; Monounsaturated fat 3g; Carbs 20g; Sodium 62mg; Dietary fiber 2g; Protein g; Cholesterol 11mg; Vitamin A 3% DV; Vitamin C 83% DV; Sugar 16g

Curried Fruit Compote

VEGAN, GLUTEN-FREE, NUT-FREE

MAKES 3 cups (serves 6) / **PREP TIME:** 20 minutes / **COOK TIME:** 10 minutes

The spicy flavor of curry is wonderful with sweet fruit. This easy recipe is full of antioxidants and fiber to help you in your quest to lower your cholesterol. Serve this compote over frozen yogurt or a thick slice of angel food cake.

1 (8-ounce) can pineapple chunks, undrained
1 ripe pear, peeled and chopped
1 Granny Smith apple, chopped
⅓ cup dried cranberries
1 cup apple juice
1 tablespoon fresh lemon juice
2 tablespoons agave nectar or packed brown sugar
1 tablespoon curry powder
1 tablespoon cornstarch
Pinch salt

1. In a medium saucepan over medium heat, combine the pineapple chunks, pear, apple, cranberries, apple juice, lemon juice, agave nectar (or brown sugar), curry powder, cornstarch, and salt. Stir to blend.

2. Bring to a boil, reduce the heat to low, and simmer for 6 to 8 minutes or until the fruit is tender.

3. At this point, you can serve the compote as-is, or you can purée all —or part—of it. The compote can be stored in the refrigerator for up to 3 days. You can rewarm the compote on the stovetop before you serve it.

INGREDIENT TIP: Agave nectar is made from the agave plant. It is vegan and has a low glycemic index, which means it won't spike your blood sugar. Some nutritionists don't like this product because it's high in fructose. Consuming too much fructose may cause resistance to leptin, a hormone related to appetite regulation and body fat storage. But eating a small amount occasionally is okay.

Per serving: Calories 112; Fat 0g (with 0% calories from fat); Saturated fat 0g; Monounsaturated fat 0g; Carbs 29g; Sodium 4mg; Dietary fiber 3g; Protein 1g; Cholesterol 0mg; Vitamin A 1% DV; Vitamin C 38% DV; Sugar 22g

Skillet Apple Crisp with Mixed Nuts

VEGETARIAN, GLUTEN-FREE

SERVES 4 / **PREP TIME:** 15 minutes / **COOK TIME:** 15 minutes

This recipe is made in two skillets—the topping is browned in one skillet as the fruit cooks down in another. Abundant fiber makes this a heart-healthy dessert choice. Feeling decadent? Serve with a dollop of vanilla frozen yogurt.

2 large Granny Smith or Gala apples, cored and sliced ½ inch thick
4 tablespoons apple juice, divided
3 tablespoons granulated sugar
2 tablespoons salted butter, divided
1 tablespoon cornstarch
¼ cup packed brown sugar
½ cup rolled oats
2 tablespoons almond flour
½ teaspoon ground cinnamon
⅛ teaspoon ground nutmeg
1 tablespoon sliced almonds
1 tablespoon chopped pecans

1. In a nonstick skillet over medium heat, combine the apples, 1 tablespoon of the apple juice, granulated sugar, and 1 tablespoon of the butter.

2. Bring the apple mixture to a simmer, reduce the heat to low, and cook for 8 to 9 minutes, stirring occasionally, until the fruit is tender.

3. In a small bowl, combine 2 tablespoons of the apple juice and the cornstarch. Stir into the apple mixture and simmer for 1 minute longer or until thickened and tender.

4. Meanwhile, in a medium bowl, combine the brown sugar, oats, almond flour, cinnamon, and nutmeg. To the oat mixture, add the remaining 1 tablespoon butter along with the remaining 3 tablespoons of the apple juice, and mix until crumbly. Stir in the almonds and pecans.

5. Put the oat mixture in another skillet over medium heat and cook until the mixture is toasted and slightly browner, about 4 to 5 minutes. Remove from the heat and transfer onto a plate.

6. When the apples are tender, top with the oat mixture and serve.

Per serving: Calories 272; Fat 11g (with 36% calories from fat); Saturated fat 5g; Monounsaturated fat 4g; Carbs 43g; Sodium 45mg; Dietary fiber 4g; Protein 3g; Cholesterol 5mg; Vitamin A 4% DV; Vitamin C 20% DV; Sugar 30g

Salted Caramel Pear and Blueberry Crisp

VEGETARIAN, NUT-FREE

SERVES 4 / **PREP TIME:** 10 minutes / **COOK TIME:** 20 minutes

Fruit crisps take a long time to bake, but making them in ramekins instead of a pie dish cuts the time down. These desserts are high in fiber and antioxidants—and rich-tasting with the addition of salted caramel sauce.

Nonstick cooking spray
2 pears, cored and chopped
1 cup fresh blueberries
2 tablespoons fresh lemon juice
¼ cup whole-wheat flour
2 tablespoons all-purpose flour
½ cup rolled oats
3 tablespoons packed brown sugar
1 teaspoon ground cinnamon
2 tablespoons butter, melted
2 tablespoons pear nectar or apple juice
2 tablespoons salted caramel sauce (see Ingredient Tip)

1. Preheat the oven to 375°F. Spray the interiors of 4 (6-ounce) ramekins or custard cups with nonstick cooking spray and place on a cookie sheet. Set aside.

2. In a small bowl, combine the pears, blueberries, and lemon juice. Divide the mixture among the ramekins.

3. In a medium bowl, combine the whole-wheat flour, all-purpose flour, oats, brown sugar, and cinnamon, and mix well.

4. In a small bowl, combine the butter and pear nectar, and mix until smooth. Drizzle over the flour mixture and stir until crumbly.

5. Drizzle the caramel sauce over the fruit in each of the ramekins and top each with some of the oat mixture. Put the ramekins on a baking sheet to catch any drips.

6. Bake the crisps for 18 to 20 minutes or until they are golden brown on top and the fruit is bubbling.

INGREDIENT TIP: There are many brands of salted caramel sauce on the market. Some good brands are Williams Sonoma, Stonewall Kitchen, and Ghirardelli.

Per serving: Calories 278; Fat 7g (with 23% calories from fat); Saturated fat 4g; Monounsaturated fat 2g; Carbs 54g; Sodium 59mg; Dietary fiber 6g; Protein 4g; Cholesterol 16mg; Vitamin A 5% DV; Vitamin C 18% DV; Sugar 25g

Chocolate Banana Caramel Pudding

VEGETARIAN, GLUTEN-FREE, NUT-FREE

SERVES 4 / **PREP TIME:** 15 minutes

Puddings usually need to be cooked, but if you start with bananas, this recipe is quick to create and ready to eat right away. Cocoa powder can help increase HDL cholesterol and help reduce LDL levels.

2 ripe bananas, cut into 1-inch chunks (see Ingredient Tip)
¼ cup cocoa powder, plus more to adjust chocolate level
¼ cup low-fat soy milk
2 tablespoons vanilla protein powder
2 tablespoons caramel sauce
½ teaspoon vanilla extract
Pinch salt
2 tablespoons mini semisweet chocolate chips

1. In a blender or food processor, combine the bananas, cocoa powder, soy milk, protein powder, caramel sauce, vanilla, and salt, and blend or process until smooth.

2. Add more cocoa, about a tablespoon at a time, if you'd like a darker chocolate pudding or to adjust the chocolate flavor.

3. Pour into 4 small cups and top each with the chocolate chips, then serve. Or you can cover the puddings and chill for 2 to 3 hours before serving.

INGREDIENT TIP: You can ripen bananas quickly if you put them into a paper bag. This causes them to release ethylene gas, which speeds up the process. The brown speckles on a ripe banana peel are a result of enzymatic browning. For this recipe you need yellow bananas with just a few spots.

Per serving: Calories 164; Fat 4g (with 22% calories from fat); Saturated fat 2g; Monounsaturated fat 1g; Carbs 25g; Sodium 29mg; Dietary fiber 4g; Protein 8g; Cholesterol 1mg; Vitamin A 4% DV; Vitamin C 9% DV; Sugar 15g

Dark Chocolate Meringues

VEGETARIAN, GLUTEN-FREE, NUT-FREE

MAKES 18 / **PREP TIME:** 15 minutes / **COOK TIME:** 15 minutes

Meringues are magical little cookies made from egg whites and sugar. They typically bake for an hour or more, but this version bakes for just 15 minutes, making a cookie that is crisp on the outside and chewy on the inside.

2 egg whites, at room temperature
⅓ cup granulated sugar
3 tablespoons confectioner's sugar
¼ cup cocoa powder
Pinch salt
½ teaspoon vanilla extract
¼ cup mini semisweet chocolate chips

1. Preheat the oven to 350°F. Line a baking sheet with parchment paper and set aside.

2. In a clean, dry medium bowl, place the egg whites. Put the bowl inside a larger bowl filled with very warm water and let stand for 5 minutes to warm up the egg whites.

3. Remove the medium bowl from the large bowl and carefully dry the outside.

4. In another medium bowl, sift together the granulated sugar, powdered sugar, cocoa powder, and salt.

5. Start beating the egg whites and gradually add the sugar mixture, beating constantly, until the mixture stands in peaks that droop when you pull up the turned-off beater.

6. Fold in the vanilla extract and the chocolate chips.

7. Drop by tablespoons onto the prepared baking sheet.

8. Bake for 13 to 15 minutes or until the meringues are set. Cool on the baking sheet for 5 minutes, then remove to a wire rack to completely cool. Store in layers separated by wax paper in an airtight container at room temperature up to 3 days.

DID YOU KNOW? Eggs will separate more easily if they are cold, but the whites beat higher if they are at room temperature. To separate egg whites, tap on the side of a bowl and pull the halves apart, keeping most of the egg in one half. Tip the egg between the two halves over a clean bowl until only the egg yolk remains in the shell. Be careful not to get any yolk into the white or it will not beat to peaks.

Per serving: Calories 35; Fat 1g (with 26% calories from fat); Saturated fat 1g; Monounsaturated fat 0g; Carbs 7g; Sodium 9mg; Dietary fiber 1g; Protein 1g; Cholesterol 0mg; Vitamin A 0% DV; Vitamin C 0% DV; Sugar 6g

Dark Chocolate Brownie Bites

VEGETARIAN, NUT-FREE

MAKES 24 bites (serves 12) / **PREP TIME:** 12 minutes / **COOK TIME:** 18 minutes

You'll need a 24 cup mini muffin pan for this indulgent recipe. Beets add sweetness and beneficial fiber to these little brownies and reduce the fat in the batter. And using canned beets is the easiest way to make puréed beets.

¼ **cup salted butter, melted**
¼ **cup puréed beets**
½ **cup packed brown sugar**
3 tablespoons honey
1 teaspoon vanilla extract
1 egg
1 egg white
Pinch salt
¼ **teaspoon baking powder**
½ **cup whole-wheat flour**
¼ **cup all-purpose flour**
⅓ **cup cocoa powder**

1. Preheat the oven to 350°F. Line 24 mini muffin cups with mini paper liners and set aside.

2. In a medium bowl, combine the butter, beets, brown sugar, honey, and vanilla and mix well.

3. Add the egg and the egg white and beat until smooth.

4. In a separate medium bowl, combine the salt, baking powder, whole-wheat flour, all-purpose flour, and cocoa powder. Stir the dry ingredients into the butter-sugar mixture just until combined.

5. Spoon the batter among the prepared muffin cups, filling each about ⅔ full. Each cup should take about 1 tablespoon of batter.

6. Bake for 16 to 18 minutes or until the little brownies are set; they will have a shiny crust. A toothpick inserted into the center will come out with moist crumbs attached. Don't overbake them or they will be hard.

7. Let the brownie bites cool for 5 minutes, then remove them to a cooling rack. You can eat these warm or cool. Store in an airtight container at room temperature up to 3 days.

Per serving: Calories 141; Fat 5g (with 32% calories from fat); Saturated fat 2g; Monounsaturated fat 1g; Carbs 22g; Sodium 51mg; Dietary fiber 2g; Protein 2g; Cholesterol 28mg; Vitamin A 3% DV; Vitamin C 0% DV; Sugar 14g

Double Chocolate Cinnamon Nice Cream

VEGAN, GLUTEN-FREE, NUT-FREE

SERVES 4 / **PREP TIME:** 15 minutes / **COOK TIME:** 5 minutes

Nice cream is the term for ice cream that is ready without freezing. This recipe uses frozen bananas, dates, and frozen mangoes, along with cocoa powder and melted chocolate chips to achieve the perfect soft-serve texture!

3 tablespoons semisweet chocolate chips
2 frozen bananas, cut into chunks
⅓ cup frozen mango cubes
2 Medjool dates, pit removed and chopped (see Ingredient Tip)
2 tablespoons flax or soy milk
3 tablespoons cocoa powder
½ teaspoon vanilla extract
½ teaspoon ground cinnamon
Pinch salt

1. In a small saucepan over low heat, melt the semisweet chocolate chips, stirring frequently. Transfer the melted chocolate from the pan to a small bowl to cool, and place it in the refrigerator while you prepare the rest of the ingredients. (Make sure to not let the chocolate harden.)

2. In a blender or food processor, combine the bananas, mangoes, dates, and milk and blend until well combined.

3. Add the cocoa powder, vanilla, cinnamon, salt, and the melted, cooled chocolate. Blend until the mixture is smooth.

4. This treat can be served right away or frozen for 2 to 3 hours before serving.

INGREDIENT TIP: Medjool dates are a premium variety of dates, with a soft texture and sweet flavor. Do not use prechopped dates in this recipe, because they are too hard and will not blend well with the other ingredients. You can also use Bahri or Dayri dates in this recipe.

Per serving: Calories 221; Fat 5g (with 20% calories from fat); Saturated fat 4g; Monounsaturated fat 3g; Carbs 40g; Sodium 8mg; Dietary fiber 6g; Protein 4g; Cholesterol 0mg; Vitamin A 6% DV; Vitamin C 23% DV; Sugar 25g

Avocado Dressing

CHAPTER TEN

Sauces and Dressings

Avocado Dressing

Chimichurri Sauce

Green Sauce

Mustard Berry Vinaigrette

Silken Fruited Tofu Cream

Zesty Citrus Kefir Dressing

Mango, Peach, and Tomato Pico de Gallo

Classic Italian Tomato Sauce

Spicy Peanut Sauce

Tzatziki

Avocado Dressing

VEGETARIAN, GLUTEN-FREE, NUT-FREE

MAKES 1½ cups (serves 8) / **PREP TIME:** 15 minutes

Avocado, with its good monounsaturated fats, makes an excellent creamy salad dressing. This recipe is one of few with a higher percentage of fat, but it's a type of healthy fat.

1 avocado, peeled and cubed
⅔ cup plain nonfat Greek yogurt
¼ cup buttermilk
2 tablespoons fresh lemon juice
1 tablespoon honey
Pinch salt
2 tablespoons chopped fresh chives
½ cup chopped cherry tomatoes

1. In a blender or food processor, combine the avocado, yogurt, buttermilk, lemon juice, honey, salt, and chives, and blend or process until smooth. Stir in the tomatoes.

2. You may need to add more buttermilk or lemon juice to achieve a pourable consistency.

3. This dressing can be stored by putting it into a small dish, then pouring about 2 teaspoons lemon juice on top. Cover the dressing by pressing plastic wrap directly onto the surface. Refrigerate for up to 1 day.

SUBSTITUTION TIP: To make this recipe vegan, substitute vegan mayonnaise for the yogurt and use water or vegetable broth in place of the buttermilk. The calories for one 2-tablespoon serving will increase to 90, and the fat content to 7 grams.

Per serving: Calories 55; Fat 3g (with 49% calories from fat); Saturated fat 1g; Monounsaturated fat 2g; Carbs 6g; Sodium 30mg; Dietary fiber 1g; Protein 2g; Cholesterol 0mg; Vitamin A 3% DV; Vitamin C 9% DV; Sugar 4g

Chimichurri Sauce

VEGAN, GLUTEN-FREE, NUT-FREE

MAKES 1 cup (serves 8) / **PREP TIME:** 15 minutes

Chimichurri sauce is typically made with a lot of oil, but we've created a lower-fat version. This recipe is delicious poured over grilled or broiled fish fillets or grilled chicken. The fresh herbs pack a flavorful punch and deliver lots of vitamin A.

1 shallot, chopped
1 garlic clove, chopped
½ cup fresh flat-leaf parsley
½ cup fresh cilantro leaves
3 tablespoons fresh basil leaves
2 tablespoons fresh lemon juice
2 tablespoons low-sodium vegetable broth
Pinch salt
⅛ teaspoon red pepper flakes

1. In a blender or food processor, add the shallot, garlic, parsley, cilantro, basil, lemon juice, vegetable broth, salt, and red pepper flakes, and process until the herbs are in tiny pieces and the mixture is well-combined.

2. Serve immediately or store in an airtight glass container in the refrigerator up to 2 days. Stir the sauce before serving.

Per serving: Calories 5; Fat 0g (with 0% calories from fat); Saturated fat 0g; Monounsaturated fat 0g; Carbs 1g; Sodium 3mg; Dietary fiber 0g; Protein 0g; Cholesterol 0mg; Vitamin A 9% DV; Vitamin C 11% DV; Sugar 0g

Green Sauce

VEGAN, GLUTEN-FREE, NUT-FREE

MAKES ½ cup (serves 4) / **PREP TIME:** 15 minutes

Most recipes for Green Sauce, which can be drizzled on everything from broiled fish to a sandwich, call for lots of avocado. This recipe uses watercress, peas, scallions, and lemon juice for a smooth and flavorful sauce with little fat.

1 cup watercress
½ cup frozen baby peas, thawed
¼ cup chopped fresh cilantro leaves
2 scallions, chopped
3 tablespoons silken tofu
2 tablespoons fresh lime juice
1 tablespoon green olive slices
1 teaspoon grated fresh lime zest
Pinch salt
Pinch white pepper

1. In a food processor or blender, combine the watercress, peas, cilantro, scallions, tofu, lime juice, olives, lime zest, salt, and white pepper, and process or blend until smooth.

2. This sauce can be used immediately, or you can store it in an airtight glass container in the refrigerator up to four days.

SUBSTITUTION TIP: You can use any type of green herb, leafy green, or green vegetable in this versatile sauce. Try cooked broccoli stems, baby spinach, parsley, edamame, or basil to make this recipe your own.

Per serving: Calories 27; Fat 1g (with 33% calories from fat); Saturated fat 0g; Monounsaturated fat 0g; Carbs 4g; Sodium 65mg; Dietary fiber 1g; Protein 2g; Cholesterol 0mg; Vitamin A 15% DV; Vitamin C 19% DV; Sugar 1g

Mustard Berry Vinaigrette

VEGAN, GLUTEN-FREE, NUT-FREE

MAKES 1 cup (serves 8) / **PREP TIME:** 10 minutes

Fresh berries add a sweet-tart flavor to this wonderful salad dressing along with vitamin C and fiber. Use it to dress any salad greens or drizzle it over baked or broiled fish or chicken.

3 tablespoons low-sodium yellow mustard
½ cup fresh raspberries
½ cup sliced fresh strawberries
2 tablespoons raspberry vinegar
2 teaspoons agave nectar
Pinch salt

1. In a blender or food processor, combine the mustard, raspberries, strawberries, raspberry vinegar, agave nectar, and salt, and blend or process until smooth. You can also combine the ingredients in a bowl and mash them with the back of a fork.

2. Store the vinaigrette in an airtight glass container in the refrigerator for up to 3 days.

INGREDIENT TIP: You can buy raspberry vinegar or make it yourself: Bring 1 cup of white vinegar to a boil, stir in 2 tablespoons sugar until dissolved. Add 1 cup raspberries, then pour the mixture into a clean glass bottle or jar. Cover tightly and let stand for a couple of days before using.

Per serving: Calories 27; Fat 0g (with 0% calories from fat); Saturated fat 0g; Monounsaturated fat 0g; Carbs 6g; Sodium 65mg; Dietary fiber 1g; Protein 0g; Cholesterol 0mg; Vitamin A 0% DV; Vitamin C 14% DV; Sugar 5g

Silken Fruited Tofu Cream

VEGAN, GLUTEN-FREE, NUT-FREE

MAKES 1¼ cups (serves 4) / **PREP TIME:** 15 minutes

This ultra-creamy, flavorful cream is a perfect complement to fresh berries or serves as a lovely dressing for any type of fruit salad. It's also delicious served as a dip with fresh fruit.

1 cup silken tofu
⅓ cup fresh raspberries
2 tablespoons orange-pineapple juice
1 tablespoon fresh lemon juice
½ teaspoon vanilla extract
⅛ teaspoon ground cinnamon
Pinch salt

1. In a blender or food processor, combine the tofu, raspberries, orange-pineapple juice, lemon juice, vanilla, cinnamon, and salt. Blend or process until smooth.

2. You can use this cream immediately or store it in an airtight glass container in the refrigerator for up to 2 days.

Per serving: Calories 49; Fat 2g (with 37% calories from fat); Saturated fat 0g; Monounsaturated fat 0g; Carbs 4g; Sodium 23mg; Dietary fiber 1g; Protein 4g; Cholesterol 0mg; Vitamin A 0% DV; Vitamin C 13% DV; Sugar 2g

Zesty Citrus Kefir Dressing

VEGETARIAN, GLUTEN-FREE, NUT-FREE

MAKES 1 cup (serves 8) / **PREP TIME:** 15 minutes

Kefir is a fermented milk drink that looks like thin yogurt. It makes a great salad dressing with citrus juices and zest. Kefir may lower LDL cholesterol too, so drizzle this recipe on your green salads.

⅔ cup kefir
2 tablespoons honey
2 tablespoons low-sodium yellow mustard
2 tablespoons fresh lemon juice
½ teaspoon fresh lemon zest
1 tablespoon fresh orange juice
½ teaspoon fresh orange zest
1 teaspoon olive oil
Pinch salt

1. In a blender or food processor, combine the kefir, honey, mustard, lemon juice and zest, orange juice and zest, olive oil, and salt. Blend or process until smooth.

2. You can serve this dressing immediately, or store it in an airtight container in the refrigerator for up to 3 days.

SUBSTITUTION TIP: If you can't kefir at your grocery store, you can substitute ½ cup plain low-fat yogurt plus 3 tablespoons low-fat milk and 1 tablespoon lemon juice.

Per serving: Calories 37; Fat 1g (with 24% calories from fat); Saturated fat 0g; Monounsaturated fat 1g; Carbs 6g; Sodium 43mg; Dietary fiber g; Protein 1g; Cholesterol 2mg; Vitamin A 1% DV; Vitamin C 5% DV; Sugar 5g

Mango, Peach, and Tomato Pico de Gallo

VEGAN, GLUTEN-FREE, NUT-FREE

MAKES 2 cups (serves 4) / **PREP TIME:** 15 minutes

Pico de gallo means "rooster's beak" in Spanish. The name may refer to the chopping of the ingredients. This type of salsa is fresh and filled with vibrant color and nutrients that are beneficial for heart health.

1 mango, peeled and cubed (see Ingredient Tip)
1 peach, peeled and chopped (see Ingredient Tip)
1 beefsteak tomato, cored and chopped
1 cup yellow or red cherry tomatoes, chopped
2 scallions, chopped
1 jalapeño pepper, seeded and minced
2 tablespoons fresh lemon juice
1 teaspoon fresh grated lemon zest
Pinch salt
⅛ teaspoon red pepper flakes

1. In a medium bowl, combine the mango, peach, tomato, scallions, jalapeño pepper, lemon juice, lemon zest, salt, and red pepper flakes, and mix well.

2. Serve immediately or store in an airtight glass container in the refrigerator for up to 2 days.

INGREDIENT TIP: To prepare a mango, first stand the fruit on end and cut it in half, working around the large flat center pit. Cup one-half in your hand, flesh up and skin down, and score the flesh with a small, sharp knife, being careful not to cut through the skin. Turn the mango inside out and slice off the cubes. Repeat with the second half.

Per serving: Calories 80; Fat 1g (with 11% calories from fat); Saturated fat 0g; Monounsaturated fat 0g; Carbs 20g; Sodium 48mg; Dietary fiber 3g; Protein 2g; Cholesterol 0mg; Vitamin A 28% DV; Vitamin C 58% DV; Sugar 14g

Classic Italian Tomato Sauce

VEGAN, GLUTEN-FREE, NUT-FREE

MAKES 2 cups (serves 4) / **PREP TIME:** 10 minutes / **COOK TIME:** 20 minutes

Classic Italian tomato sauce is made with fresh tomatoes; plum tomatoes are the best because they are dense. This recipe uses tomato skin because that is where most of the flavonols (that help reduce LDL cholesterol) are found.

2 teaspoons olive oil
1 onion, chopped
3 cloves garlic, minced
1½ pounds plum (Roma) tomatoes, chopped
2 tablespoons no-salt-added tomato paste
2 tablespoons finely grated carrot
1 teaspoon dried basil leaves
½ teaspoon dried oregano
⅛ teaspoon white pepper
Pinch salt
Pinch sugar
2 tablespoons fresh basil leaves, chopped

1. In a large saucepan, heat the olive oil over medium heat.

2. Add the onion and garlic, and cook and stir for 3 minutes or until the onions are translucent.

3. Add the tomatoes, tomato paste, carrot, basil, oregano, white pepper, salt, and sugar, and stir and bring to a simmer.

4. Simmer for 15 to 18 minutes, stirring frequently, or until the sauce thickens slightly.

5. Stir in the fresh basil and serve.

Per serving: Calories 73; Fat 3g (with 37% calories from fat); Saturated fat 0g; Monounsaturated fat 0g; Carbs 13g; Sodium 19mg; Dietary fiber 3g; Protein 2g; Cholesterol 0mg; Vitamin A 38% DV; Vitamin C 44% DV; Sugar 7g

Spicy Peanut Sauce

VEGETARIAN, GLUTEN-FREE

MAKES 1 cup (serves 8) / **PREP TIME:** 15 minutes

This smooth and spicy sauce can be used many ways: as a dip for vegetables, as a sauce for grilled fish or chicken, and thinned with more lime juice, as a salad dressing. The trick is to use powdered peanut butter, which lowers the fat content.

½ cup powdered peanut butter (see Ingredient Tip)
2 tablespoons reduced-fat peanut butter
⅓ cup plain nonfat Greek yogurt
2 tablespoons fresh lime juice
2 teaspoons low-sodium soy sauce
1 scallion, chopped
1 clove garlic, minced
1 jalapeño pepper, seeded and minced
⅛ teaspoon red pepper flakes

1. In a blender or food processor, combine powdered peanut butter, reduced-fat peanut butter, yogurt, lime juice, soy sauce, scallion, garlic, jalapeño pepper, and red pepper flakes, and blend or process until smooth.

2. Serve immediately or store in an airtight glass container and refrigerate for up to 3 days. You can thin this sauce with more lime juice if necessary.

INGREDIENT TIP: Powdered peanut butter may seem like a highly processed food, but it's just made from peanuts with the oil removed. It has the same protein and fiber as regular peanut butter. Read the label to make sure the powdered peanut butter you buy doesn't have any added salt or sugar. This product is easy to find online.

Per serving: Calories 60; Fat 3g (with 45% calories from fat); Saturated fat 0g; Monounsaturated fat 1g; Carbs 5g; Sodium 88mg; Dietary fiber 0g; Protein 6g; Cholesterol 2mg; Vitamin A 1% DV; Vitamin C 5% DV; Sugar 2g

Tzatziki

VEGETARIAN, GLUTEN-FREE, NUT-FREE

MAKES 2 cups (serves 4) / **PREP TIME:** 30 minutes

This cool and soothing sauce comes from Greece, where it is typically served with fish. It can be served as a dip with vegetables, or as a salad dressing if it's thinned with buttermilk or lemon juice.

1¼ cups plain low-fat Greek yogurt
1 cucumber, peeled, seeded, and diced
2 tablespoons fresh lime juice
½ teaspoon grated fresh lime zest
2 cloves garlic, minced
Pinch salt
⅛ teaspoon white pepper
1 tablespoon minced fresh dill
1 tablespoon minced fresh mint
2 teaspoons olive oil

1. In a medium bowl, combine the yogurt, cucumber, lime juice, lime zest, garlic, salt, white pepper, dill, and mint.

2. Transfer the mixture to a serving bowl. Drizzle with the olive oil.

3. Serve immediately or store in an airtight glass container and refrigerate for up to 2 days.

Per serving: Calories 100; Fat 4g (with 32% calories from fat); Saturated fat 1g; Monounsaturated fat 2g; Carbs 11g; Sodium 56mg; Dietary fiber 1g; Protein 5g; Cholesterol 6mg; Vitamin A 3% DV; Vitamin C 11% DV; Sugar 7g

The Dirty Dozen and the Clean Fifteen™

A nonprofit environmental watchdog organization called Environmental Working Group (EWG) looks at data supplied by the US Department of Agriculture (USDA) and the Food and Drug Administration (FDA) about pesticide residues. Each year it compiles a list of the best and worst pesticide loads found in commercial crops. You can use these lists to decide which fruits and vegetables to buy organic to minimize your exposure to pesticides and which produce is considered safe enough to buy conventionally. This does not mean they are pesticide-free, though, so wash these fruits and vegetables thoroughly. The list is updated annually, and you can find it online at EWG.org/FoodNews.

Dirty Dozen™

1. strawberries
2. spinach
3. kale
4. nectarines
5. apples
6. grapes
7. peaches
8. cherries
9. pears
10. tomatoes
11. celery
12. potatoes

†Additionally, nearly three-quarters of hot pepper samples contained pesticide residues.

Clean Fifteen™

1. avocados
2. sweet corn*
3. pineapples
4. sweet peas (frozen)

5. onions
6. papayas*
7. eggplants
8. asparagus
9. kiwis
10. cabbages
11. cauliflower
12. cantaloupes
13. broccoli
14. mushrooms
15. honeydew melons

* A small amount of sweet corn, papaya, and summer squash sold in the United States is produced from genetically modified seeds. Buy organic varieties of these crops if you want to avoid genetically modified produce.

Measurement Conversions

VOLUME EQUIVALENTS (LIQUID)

US STANDARD	US STANDARD (OUNCES)	METRIC (APPROXIMATE)
2 tablespoons	1 fl. oz.	30 mL
¼ cup	2 fl. oz.	60 mL
½ cup	4 fl. oz.	120 mL
1 cup	8 fl. oz.	240 mL
1½ cups	12 fl. oz.	355 mL
2 cups or 1 pint	16 fl. oz.	475 mL
4 cups or 1 quart	32 fl. oz.	1 L
1 gallon	128 fl. oz.	4 L

OVEN TEMPERATURES

FAHRENHEIT	CELSIUS (APPROXIMATE)
250°F	120°C
300°F	150°C
325°F	165°C
350°F	180°C
375°F	190°C
400°F	200°C
425°F	220°C
450°F	230°C

VOLUME EQUIVALENTS (DRY)

US STANDARD	METRIC (APPROXIMATE)
⅛ teaspoon	0.5 mL
¼ teaspoon	1 mL
½ teaspoon	2 mL
¾ teaspoon	4 mL
1 teaspoon	5 mL
1 tablespoon	15 mL
¼ cup	59 mL
⅓ cup	79 mL
½ cup	118 mL
⅔ cup	156 mL
¾ cup	177 mL
1 cup	235 mL
2 cups or 1 pint	475 mL
3 cups	700 mL
4 cups or 1 quart	1 L

WEIGHT EQUIVALENTS

US STANDARD	METRIC (APPROXIMATE)
½ ounce	15 g
1 ounce	30 g
2 ounces	60 g
4 ounces	115 g
8 ounces	225 g
12 ounces	340 g
16 ounces or 1 pound	455 g

Understanding Cholesterol

The following health authorities discuss cholesterol in more detail:

American Heart Association

"About Cholesterol."
https://www.heart.org/en/health-topics/cholesterol/about-cholesterol.
"Prevention and Treatment of High Cholesterol (Hyperlipidemia)."
https://www.heart.org/en/health-topics/cholesterol/prevention-and-treatment-of-high-cholesterol-hyperlipidemia.
"2018 Guideline on the Management of Blood Cholesterol."
https://professional.heart.org/professional/ScienceNews/UCM_502791_2018-Cholesterol-Management-Guideline.jsp.

National Heart, Lung, and Blood Institute

"High Blood Cholesterol." https://www.nhlbi.nih.gov/health-topics/high-blood-cholesterol.

Centers for Disease Control and Prevention

"LDL and HDL Cholesterol: 'Bad' and 'Good' Cholesterol."
https://www.cdc.gov/cholesterol/ldl_hdl.htm.

Mayo Clinic

"High Cholesterol." https://www.mayoclinic.org/diseases-conditions/high-blood-cholesterol/symptoms-causes/syc-20350800.

"Triglycerides: Why Do They Matter?"
https://www.mayoclinic.org/diseases-conditions/high-blood-cholesterol/in-depth/triglycerides/art-20048186.

Cleveland Clinic

"Cholesterol Numbers: What Do They Mean."
https://my.clevelandclinic.org/health/articles/11920-cholesterol-numbers-what-do-they-mean.

10-Year Heart Disease Risk Calculator

If you are over 40 and don't already take a statin or have heart disease, you can use the easy, online Atherosclerotic Cardiovascular Disease (ASCVD) Risk Calculator to assess your personal 10-year risk of heart disease. All you need is your cholesterol test results and your blood pressure. It takes just minutes and you'll be rewarded with results you can discuss with your doctor.

Access the American College of Cardiology's ASCVD Risk Estimator Plus here (it's even available as a downloadable app):

http://tools.acc.org/ASCVD-Risk-Estimator-Plus/#!/calculate/estimate.

Eating to Lower Cholesterol

The following health authorities provide detailed information about eating to lower cholesterol:

American Heart Association

"Cooking to Lower Cholesterol." https://www.heart.org/en/health-topics/cholesterol/prevention-and-treatment-of-high-cholesterol-hyperlipidemia/cooking-to-lower-cholesterol.

"Whole Grains, Refined Grains, and Dietary Fiber."
www.heart.org/en/healthy-living/healthy-eating/eat-smart/nutrition-basics/whole-grains-refined-grains-and-dietary-fiber.

National Heart, Lung, and Blood Institute

"High Blood Cholesterol: Heart-Healthy Lifestyle Changes."
https://www.nhlbi.nih.gov/health-topics/high-blood-cholesterol.

Harvard Health Publishing, Harvard Medical School

"11 Foods that Lower Cholesterol." www.health.harvard.edu/heart-health/11-foods-that-lower-cholesterol.

"How to Lower Your Cholesterol Without Drugs."
www.health.harvard.edu/heart-health/how-to-lower-your-cholesterol-without-drugs.

Mayo Clinic

"Cholesterol: Top Foods to Improve Your Numbers."
www.mayoclinic.org/diseases-conditions/high-blood-cholesterol/in-depth/cholesterol/art-20045192.

References

The sources listed in this section follow the sequence of the text and headings of chapter 1.

Sidebar: A Closer Look at Cholesterol Levels

National Heart, Lung, and Blood Institute. "High Blood Cholesterol." Accessed April 22, 2019. www.nhlbi.nih.gov/health-topics/high-blood-cholesterol.

Mayo Clinic. "Triglycerides: Why Do They Matter." Accessed April 22, 2019. www.mayoclinic.org/diseases-conditions/high-blood-cholesterol/in-depth/triglycerides/art-20048186.

American Heart Association. "Understand Your Risks to Prevent a Heart Attack." Accessed April 22, 2019. www.heart.org/en/health-topics/heart-attack/understand-your-risks-to-prevent-a-heart-attack.

Low-Cholesterol Eating Principles

American Heart Association. "Prevention and Treatment of High Cholesterol (Hyperlipidemia)." Accessed April 23, 2019. www.heart.org/en/health-topics/cholesterol/prevention-and-treatment-of-high-cholesterol-hyperlipidemia.

Office of Disease Prevention and Health Promotion. "2015 to 2020 Dietary Guidelines for Americans." Accessed April 23, 2019. www.health.gov/dietaryguidelines/2015.

National Lipid Association. "Adding Soluble Fiber to Lower Your Cholesterol." Accessed June 2, 2019.

www.lipid.org/sites/default/files/adding_soluble_fiber_final_0.pdf.

CardioSmart. "Experts Clarify Definition of a Heart-Healthy Diet." Accessed April 23, 2019. www.cardiosmart.org/News-and-Events/2016/11/Experts-Clarify-Definition-of-a-HeartHealthy-Diet.

American Heart Association. "Mediterranean Diet." Accessed April 23, 2019. https://www.heart.org/en/healthy-living/healthy-eating/eat-smart/nutrition-basics/mediterranean-diet.

CardioSmart. "High Cholesterol: The TLC Diet." Accessed April 23, 2019. www.cardiosmart.org/~/media/Documents/Fact%20Sheets/en/abk6159.ashx.

Office of Disease Prevention and Health Promotion. "2015 to 2020 Dietary Guidelines for Americans: Appendix 13. Food Sources of Dietary Fiber." Accessed April 23, 2019. www.health.gov/dietaryguidelines/2015/guidelines/appendix-13.

Mayo Clinic. "Cholesterol: Top Foods to Improve Your Numbers." Accessed April 25, 2019. www.mayoclinic.org/diseases-conditions/high-blood-cholesterol/in-depth/cholesterol/art-20045192.

WebMD. "Top 10 Sources of Fiber." Accessed April 23, 2019. www.webmd.com/diet/features/top-10-sources-of-fiber.

American Heart Association. "Whole Grains, Refined Grains, and Dietary Fiber." Accessed April 25, 2019. www.heart.org/en/healthy-living/healthy-eating/eat-smart/nutrition-basics/whole-grains-refined-grains-and-dietary-fiber.

Healthline. "Top 20 Foods High in Soluble Fiber." Accessed April 25, 2019. www.healthline.com/nutrition/foods-high-in-soluble-fiber.

MedlinePlus. "Soluble vs. Insoluble Fiber." Accessed April 25, 2019. www.medlineplus.gov/ency/article/002136.htm.

Diet Guidelines

National Heart, Lung, and Blood Institute. "Your Guide to Lowering Your Cholesterol with TLC." Accessed April 23, 2019. www.nhlbi.nih.gov/files/docs/public/heart/chol_tlc.pdf.

U.S. Department of Agriculture. "Food Data Central Search Results." Accessed April 23, 2019. https://fdc.nal.usda.gov/fdc-app.html#/food-details/170720/nutrients

American Heart Association. "The American Heart Association Diet and Lifestyle Recommendations." Accessed April 23, 2019. https://www.heart.org/en/healthy-living/healthy-eating/eat-smart/nutrition-basics/aha-diet-and-lifestyle-recommendations.

Recommended Daily Dietary Cholesterol

Mayo Clinic. "Eggs: Are They Good or Bad for My Cholesterol?" Accessed April 23, 2019. www.mayoclinic.org/diseases-conditions/high-blood-cholesterol/expert-answers/cholesterol/faq-20058468.

The Diet Connection

Supplements

Pritikin Longevity Center & Spa. "Lowering Cholesterol Naturally—6 Tips." Accessed April 24, 2019. www.pritikin.com/your-health/health-benefits/lower-cholesterol/1468-7-tips-for-improving-your-ldl-cholesterol.html.

National Center for Complementary and Integrative Health. "5 Tips: What You Should Know About High Blood Cholesterol." Accessed April 24, 2019. www.nccih.nih.gov/health/tips/cholesterol.

Health. "Cholesterol-Lowering Supplements: What Works, What Doesn't." Accessed April 24, 2019. www.health.com/health/condition-article/0,,20295990,00.html.

Berkeley Wellness. "Cholesterol Lowering Supplements." Accessed April 24, 2019. www.berkeleywellness.com/supplements/other-supplements/lists/cholesterol-lowering-supplements/slideid_474.

WebMD. "Supplement Smarts for Cholesterol and Triglycerides." Accessed April 24, 2019. www.webmd.com/cholesterol-management/supplements#1.

American Heart Association. "Whole Grains, Refined Grains, and Dietary Fiber." Accessed April 24, 2019. www.heart.org/en/healthy-living/healthy-eating/eat-smart/nutrition-basics/whole-grains-refined-grains-and-dietary-fiber.

National Center for Biotechnology Information. "Effect of Whey Protein on Blood Lipid Profiles: a Meta-Analysis of Randomized Controlled Trials." Accessed April 24, 2019. www.ncbi.nlm.nih.gov/pubmed/27026427.

Mayo Clinic. "Cholesterol: Top Foods to Improve Your Numbers." Accessed April 24, 2019. www.mayoclinic.org/diseases-conditions/high-blood-cholesterol/in-depth/cholesterol/art-20045192.

Cleveland Clinic. "Phytosterols: Sterols & Stanols." Accessed April 24, 2019. https://my.clevelandclinic.org/health/articles/17368-phytosterols-sterols—stanols.

Medical News Today. "Seven Benefits of Psyllium." Accessed June 24, 2019. www.medicalnewstoday.com/articles/318707.php.

Cardiovascular Business. "AHA Does Not Recommend Omega-3 Fish Oil Supplements to Prevent Heart Disease." Accessed April 24, 2019." www.cardiovascularbusiness.com/topics/practice-management/aha-does-not-recommend-omega-3-fish-oil-supplements-prevent-heart.

National Center for Complementary and Integrative Health. "Red Yeast Rice." Accessed June 24, 2019. www.nccih.nih.gov/health/redyeastrice.

Circulation. "Omega-3 Polyunsaturated Fatty Acid (Fish Oil) Supplementation and the Prevention of Clinical Cardiovascular Disease." Accessed April 24, 2019. www.ahajournals.org/doi/full/10.1161/CIR.0000000000000482.

Exercise

American Heart Association. "American Heart Association Recommendations for Physical Activity in Adults." Accessed April 23, 2019. https://www.heart.org/HEARTORG/HealthyLiving/PhysicalActivity/StartWalking/American-Heart-Association-Guidelines-for-Physical-Activity_UCM_307976_Article.jsp.

American Heart Association. "What Exercise Is Right for Me?" Accessed April 23, 2019. www.heart.org/en/healthy-living/go-red-get-fit/what-exercise-is-right-for-me?s=q%253Dmoderate%252520to%252520vigorous%252520exercise%2526sort%253Drelevancy.

Centers For Disease Control and Prevention. "General Physical Activities Defined by Level of Intensity." Accessed April 23, 2019. www.cdc.gov/nccdphp/dnpa/physical/pdf/pa_intensity_table_2_1.pdf.

American Heart Association. "Strength and Resistance Training Exercise." Accessed April 23, 2019. www.heart.org/en/healthy-living/fitness/fitness-basics/strength-and-resistance-training-exercise.

American Heart Association. "Cholesterol Management Guide For Healthcare Practitioners." Accessed April 23, 2019. www.heart.org/-/media/files/health-topics/cholesterol/chlstrmngmntgd_181110.pdf.

Cholesterol Fighters

Mayo Clinic. "Cholesterol: Top Foods to Improve Your Numbers." Accessed April 24, 2019. www.mayoclinic.org/diseases-conditions/high-blood-cholesterol/in-depth/cholesterol/art-20045192.

Cleveland Clinic. "Heart Healthy Benefits of Chocolate." Accessed April 24, 2019. https://my.clevelandclinic.org/health/articles/16774-heart-healthy-benefits-of-chocolate.

American Heart Association. "An Avocado A Day May Keep Bad Cholesterol At Bay." Accessed April 24, 2019. www.heart.org/en/news/2018/05/01/an-avocado-a-day-may-help-keep-bad-cholesterol-at-bay.

Harvard Health Publishing Harvard Medical School. "11 Foods that Lower Cholesterol." Accessed April 24, 2019. www.health.harvard.edu/heart-health/11-foods-that-lower-cholesterol.

Eating Out with High Cholesterol

Cleveland Clinic. "Cholesterol Guide: Eating Out." Accessed April 25, 2019. https://my.clevelandclinic.org/health/diseases/12109-cholesterol-guide-eating-out.

Everyday Health. "Healthy Dining Out with High Cholesterol." Accessed April 25, 2019. https://www.everydayhealth.com/high-cholesterol/living-with/dining-out-with-high-cholesterol.

Welchol ADDvantage Program. "Healthy Eating Out. Tips On Healthy, Low Cholesterol Foods When You're Out to Eat." Accessed April 24, 2019. http://welcholaddvantageprogram.com/eating-out.

WebMD. "High Cholesterol: Healthy Choices When Eating Out." Accessed April 25, 2019. www.webmd.com/cholesterol-management/healthy-choices-when-eating-out.

Self. "The 17 Healthiest Chinese Food Takeout Options, According to Registered Dietitians." Accessed April 25, 2019. www.self.com/story/registered-dietitians-order-chinese-takeout.

SF Gate. "Is Sushi a Heart Smart Food?" Accessed April 25, 2019. https://healthyeating.sfgate.com/sushi-heart-smart-food-1774.html.

WebMD. "Best & Worst Sushi for Your Health." Accessed April 25, 2019. www.webmd.com/diet/ss/slideshow-best-worst-sushi-health.

WebMD. "Best & Worst Indian Dishes for Your Health." Accessed April 25, 2019. www.webmd.com/diet/ss/slideshow-diet-best-worst-indian.

Printed in Great Britain
by Amazon

26377168R00183